Philosophical Issues in Education:
An Introduction

2011

Philosophical Issues in Education:
An Introduction

Cornel M. Hamm

 **RoutledgeFalmer**
Taylor & Francis Group

LONDON AND NEW YORK

First published 1989

Reprinted 2003
by RoutledgeFalmer
11 New Fetter Lane
London EC4P 4EE

RoutledgeFalmer is an imprint of the Taylor & Francis Group

Transferred to Digital Printing 2004

British Library Cataloguing in Publication Data

Hamm, Cornel M.
  Philosophical issues in education: an introduction
  1. Philosophy of education
  I. Title
  370'.1   1005299187

  ISBN 1-85000-598-2
  ISBN 1-85000-599-0   pbk

Library of Congress Cataloging-in-Publication Data

Hamm, Cornel M.
    Philosophical issues in education:
  an introduction/Cornel M. Hamm.
    p. cm.
  Includes index.
  ISBN 1-85000-598-2. — ISBN 1-85000-599-0 (pbk.)
  1. Education — Philosophy. 2. Education —
  Aims and objectives. I. Title.
  LB885.H28P48 1989
  370'.1 — dc20   89-11659
                                                       CIP

Jacket design by Caroline Archer
Printed and bound by Antony Rowe Ltd, Eastbourne

Table of Contents

Acknowledgments   *vii*

Introduction   *ix*

CHAPTER 1   The Nature of Philosophical Inquiry into
              Educational Discourse   1
                  What is Philosophy of Education?   1
                  Definitions and the Problem of Meaning   10

CHAPTER 2   Metaphors in Educational Discourse   18
                  Pitfalls of Language — Vagueness, Ambiguity,
                      Emotive Uses   18
                  Metaphorical Language   19
                  Analyzing Educational Metaphors   20

CHAPTER 3   An Analysis of the Concept of Education   29
                  Several Uses of the Term 'Education'   29
                  R.S. Peters' Analysis of 'Education'   32
                  Critical Remarks on Peters' Criteria   39

CHAPTER 4   'Aims' in Education   44
                  The Logic of 'Aim'   44
                  Development of Persons as the Aim of
                      Education   45
                  Interpreting 'Aims of Education'   50
                  The Role of the School in Society   53

CHAPTER 5   Educational Curricula and the Nature of
              Knowledge   59
                  The Concept 'Curriculum'   59
                  Elements of Curriculum   60
                  The Nature of Knowledge   62

Table of Contents

	The Differentiation of Knowledge	67
	Criticism of Hirst's 'Forms of Knowledge'	71
CHAPTER 6	Child-Centered Curricula	76
	Contrasting Approaches to Curriculum	76
	The 'Needs' Curriculum	78
	Human Nature Considerations	83
	Principles for Selecting Curriculum Content	88
CHAPTER 7	Teaching and Learning and Education	91
	The Concept 'Learning'	91
	The Concept 'Teaching'	93
	Relationships Between Education, Teaching, and Learning	96
	Indoctrination and Other Forms of Miseducation	99
CHAPTER 8	Inter-personal and Social Issues in Education	108
	Discipline	108
	Punishment	111
	Freedom and Authority	118
	The Student-Teacher Relationship	123
CHAPTER 9	Moral Education	128
	Introduction: Why Moral Education?	128
	Moral Education and Values Education	129
	Moral Development as the Achievement of Virtue	129
	The Paradox of Moral Education	158
CHAPTER 10	The Justification of Education	163
	The Nature of the Justification	163
	Kinds of Justification	165
	A Moral Argument	165
	Instrumental Justification	166
	The Pleasure Principle as Justification	167
	Non-Instrumental (Intrinsic) Justification	169
Bibliography		176
Index		181

Acknowledgments

Readers of this text who are familiar with the work of R.S. Peters and P.H. Hirst will immediately recognize my great indebtedness to them. To Richard Peters, my former mentor and advisor, I owe many ideas and the major orientation of this book, but particularly Chapters 3 and 10 and parts of Chapter 4 and 9. My debt to him is, however, larger than merely academic. For his inspiration, encouragement, and friendship over the years I am deeply appreciative and grateful.

Hardly less influential has been Paul Hirst, where teaching and writing have left and indelible mark in my thinking about education. Most recently he read and commented upon, and helped me improve, Chapter 5 of this text. For his encouragement and the permission to replicate his work I am most thankful.

Others, whose work is incorporated into this text and who offered encouragement and permission to replicate their work are: Israel Scheffler (parts of Chapter 1 and 2); Robert Dearden (parts of Chapter 6); Keith Fleming (part of Chapter 7); and Tasos Kazepides (parts of Chapter 7 and 8). I want to thank them and also *Melbourne Studies in Education* for granting me permission to reprint the greater part of my paper 'Moral Education as the Achievement of Virtue' (1985 *Melbourne Studies in Education*...) which now constitutes a large part of Chapter 9 in this next.

A special kind of gratitude I owe to Donald Maclean, who not only read the entire version of an early draft and helped prevent infelicities and horrible howlers but also encouraged me by discussing and debating content. Even more important, he, as a fellow teacher in earlier times, modeled excellent educational practice and critical thought about practice, which played a large part in my pursuit of philosophy of education in the first place.

Introduction

This introductory book in philosophy of education has been produced for the beginning student in the discipline. No previous experience in formal studies in either philosophy or education is a requirement for a full comprehension of the text. It is a product of the author's experience over a number of years of offering elementary courses in philosophy of education to first and second year college and university students who had either a general interest in the study of education or a more specific interest in becoming teachers. This text is suitable for both such groups and would therefore be useable in Departments of Philosophy as well as Faculties of Education.

Philosophy of education is a relative newcomer to the scene of academic disciplines. Only in the last few decades has philosophy of education become known and accepted as a specific branch of general philosophy and that primarily in Britain. The methodological stance taken in the new discipline is a synthesis of the tools of modern philosophical analysis, yielding rigourous thought and clarity of meaning, and the more traditional concern with examination of factual claims and justification of values, producing better arguments for decision-making in the practical world of education.

The features of this text which differentiate it from other modern texts in the field are: clarity, completeness, and currency.

Many of the ideas in this text have been expressed elsewhere in a manner which students find difficult to grasp. These same ideas are expressed here simply and clearly without sacrificing the rigour necessary for understanding complex philosophical matters. This is achieved by the elimination of unnecessary philosophical jargon, by minimal reference to other philosophers, by the use of tables and diagrams when appropriate, and by use of plain language and coherent organization of ideas.

The text also aims at completeness in so far as that is possible in a text of this kind. It is unlikely that there could be a 'complete' introduction to any field of study since the very notion of introduction suggests incompleteness. The attempt, then, is merely to broaden the range of topics for discussion to a degree that is wider than in some other texts of merit. In P.H. Hirst's and R.S. Peter's *The Logic of Education* (Routledge and Kegan Paul, 1970), for example; there is no attempt to provide 'an exhaustive treatment of the issues' (p. 15). Some topics included in the present text which are omitted in *The Logic of Education* are sections on metaphors in educational discourse, 'aims' in education, moral education, and the justification of education. The reader of the present work will nevertheless detect a significant overlap of content and ideas with *The Logic of Education* on topics common to both. The justification for such similarity of coverage is that students, at least on the North American side of the Atlantic, find the Hirst and Peters text difficult to read and understand. The two texts can be used (and on a trial basis have most successfully been used) as companion texts in introductory courses in philosophy of education.

The present volume also attempts to be current. Though there is no attempt to search out and follow fashionable trends, there is here an honest effort to take into account up-to-date arguments which are thought by the author to be the best available on the topics under discussion. The temptation is to say that the book is more correct on a number of issues than are other books. That, however, must be for the reader to judge, for in philosophy there usually is no final correct answer. The text then must be taken as yet another considered point of view on difficult and disputable educational concerns. At the very least, it is yet another approach to the perennial issues in philosophy of education expressed in a manner to enable beginning students to grasp the issues more clearly and as a result be encouraged to pursue them further in greater depth.

Cornel Hamm
Vancouver, 1989

CHAPTER 1

The Nature of Philosophical Inquiry into Educational Discourse

Most adults at some time or other philosophize about education; but most of them do not do so often enough and well enough. To help them think philosophically about educational matters better and more often is one of the main purposes of this book. So the book begins with a discussion of the nature of philosophical inquiries into education in the hope that the reader will become more aware of what philosophical thought is like and as a result engage in it more deliberately and competently. This first chapter focuses on the nature of philosophy of education and how philosophical study can help solve the burgeoning problem of meaning in educational discourse. The second chapter focuses on the use of metaphors in educational language as attempts to gain understanding of the nature of education. The two chapters together help to show how the remaining parts of the book proceed and how philosophy is done and seen to be invaluable in educational studies.

What is Philosophy of Education?

To understand what philosophy of education is, it is necessary to gain an understanding of what philosophy is, since philosophy of education is simply philosophy about education. As such it can be thought of as a branch of the discipline of general philosophy. Not all serious thinkers about education would agree that philosophy of education is a branch of philosophy; and a number of people who have called themselves 'philosophers of education' doing 'philosophy of education' are engaged in activities other than, and only peripherally to, what is here considered philosophy of education. So perhaps the best way to start to clarify what philosophy of education is, is to state what it is not.

Distinguishing Educational Theory from Philosophy of Education

First, philosophy of education is not synonymous with educational theory. Many practically-minded people in schools and faculties of education have thought long and hard and well about educational aims, curricular content and implementation, teaching and classroom strategies, and come up with a theory, or system, of education around which they plan their activities. What this system or theory includes are elements of various disciplines such as psychology (When do children best learn generalizations or abstractions?), sociology (What is the social impact of having separate schools for boys and girls?), organizational theory (What is the ideal role of the school principal?), and other disciplines, including philosophy (In what sense is a school an *educational* institution as distinct from a place for *training* people?) Most people have theories of education in the above sense, some more thorough and factually secure than others. And we all should, and particularly educators should, have sound theories of education. But building theories of education is not doing philosophy of education. And those who have 'progressive', or 'monitorial', or 'Herbartian', or 'wholeness', or 'child-centered' *philosophies* of education are using 'philosophy' in a sense almost equivalent to the notion of theory under discussion. Philosophy of education as understood here is only one necessary element of educational theory.

Philosophy of education also is not a study of the history of educational thought. In some circles what passes as philosophy of education is really only a study of the thought of so-called 'great educators' or of other serious thinkers about education, particularly those thinkers who are philosophers in their own right such as Plato, Locke, or Kant. Often these thoughts, however, are merely the statements of the individual's ideals in education and favourite prescriptions for child rearing. Interesting though some of these ideas are, they are not necessarily philosophical in kind, nor do the thinkers arrive at their beliefs by reasoning philosophically. Writers such as Comenius, Rousseau, Pestalozzi, Froebel, Montessori, and Dewey say interesting things about a variety of topics roughly related to education such as experimentation, play, nature, instinct, democracy, freedom, harmony, wholeness and so on. Yet often these thoughts are conceptually crude and confused, highly speculative, unfounded or contradictory. At other times they are startlingly clear and factually sound but not philosophical. Even when first-rate philosophers, such as Kant and Rousseau, write on education, they often fail to be philosophical about the issues connected with education.

Philosophy of education, furthermore, is not a matter of drawing conclusions, making extrapolations, and eliciting implications from bodies of systematic and doctrinaire thought of a metaphysical, social-political, or religious nature. Such an activity can be thought of as the 'isms' approach to philosophy of education. This sort of activity was predominant in courses in 'philosophy of education' in times past, particularly in the United States. In some institutions this is still going on and some books on the topic still organize their material in this fashion. M.L. Bigge, in *Educational Philosophies for Teachers*,[1] for example, has chapter titles based on topics such as idealism, realism, theism, empiricism, existentialism, and experimentalism. Others might include in such list of topics Marxism, Thomism, liberalism, humanism, secularism, pragmatism, phenomenalism, classicism, essentialism. These various 'isms' take a particular position on a variety of highly speculative issues and attempt to build some sort of practical educational system around the core ideas. In this they resemble the educational theorists discussed briefly above, though they are even less concerned with philosophical method and rigour. Many of the core ideas are highly questionable and the implications drawn from them extremely weak and tenuous. Modern philosophy of education fortunately has turned away from this type of enterprise.

Turning now to what philosophy of education is, it is well to remind ourselves how we began by noting that philosophy of education is a branch of philosophy and that to get a grip on how philosophers of education think and function one must become clear on what philosophy itself is. That will not be an easy task because what philosophy as such is, is itself highly controversial and difficult to define. In the discussion to follow we may not be able to remove all the problems surrounding the controversy nor clearly to define philosophy, but we can to a considerable extent move in that direction.

The Many Uses of 'Philosophy'

One of the problems concerning the nature of philosophy in general is that the term 'philosophy' is used in many different non-professional senses. Thus we read in the newspaper about 'the Queen's philosophy of horse racing', or 'the philanderer's philosophy of love', or 'the school teacher's philosophy of spelling'. In these examples, the term 'philosophy' could without loss of meaning be replaced with a term similar to 'considered view about'. But of course not every considered view is philosophical or the result of philosophizing. So these examples do very little to help us understand what professional philosophers mean by the term. At other times we say things like, 'Be more philosophical!' to someone in an excited or emotional state with the intent that the person take a more relaxed, detached, and reflective view of a situation. Here again we have a use of 'philosophy' that does not help us to understand what philosophers do when they philosophize. And there are numerous other such uses.

But even when philosophers attempt to define what it is they do when they philosophize, they often do not agree on how ideally they should proceed nor how to define precisely what it is they do even when they agree roughly on how to proceed. To think of philosophy as the search for and dispensing of wisdom, a view derived from the Greek meaning of the word 'philosophy' ('love of wisdom') is mistaken in that it claims far too much for philosophy and philosophers. Many people who are wise are not philosophers and many good philosophers are not wise. To think of philosophers as lovers of wisdom rather than achievers of wisdom is perhaps more appropriate, emphasizing as it does method or approach to certain problems rather than emphasizing a product or a body of knowledge and prescriptions for wise living. Other definitions of 'philosophy' often suffer the same fate; they allude to aspects of philosophy which are either not necessary or not sufficient. Bertrand Russell's view of philosophy as persistent attempt at clearheadedness is deficient in that clearheadedness certainly is necessary for doing philosophy, but it is not sufficient. One would hope that many people, including pilots, doctors, and nuclear scientists, would be consistently clearheaded in their concerns, but that does not mean that they are therefore doing philosophy. A view alleged to be Wittgenstein's, that philosophy is a form of language therapy in which idle language is put back to work through a process of conceptual clarification, errs in the opposite direction. The form of conceptual analysis suggested is a sufficient condition for doing philosophy, but it is not necessary. There are philosophical concerns that go beyond clarity and analysis. Other philosophers think of philosophy as a second-order activity, or taking the stance of a Martian. The main idea alluded to in these analogies is that philosophical thought and language is about our ordinary ways of thinking and speaking; it is language about language or thought about thought. Thus P.H. Hirst writes: 'It is a rather distinctive type of higherorder pursuit, primarily an analytic pursuit, with the ambition of understanding the concepts used in all other forms of lower-order knowledge and awareness . . . of our primary forms of understanding . . . in the sciences, in morals, in history and the like'.[2] Philosophy thus starts at the common sense level of thought and eventually forces one to think at levels beyond the ordinary. Thoughts such as these prompt one to offer the suggestion that philosophy is an uncommon amount of common sense. But this too is only a necessary, not a sufficient, condition; though it does help to make the point that philosophy is not a mysterious discipline trafficking in esoteric and difficult ideas that only a brilliant few are capable of understanding. Other definitions offered, such as: 'Philosophy is the pursuit of truth', '. . . is the search for the meaning of life', '. . . is that which deals with ultimate reality', and so on, all fail to transmit satisfactorily to the uninitiated a knowledge and understanding of philosophy. In sum, one or two short-sentence definitions *by themselves* inevitably fail to convey the full meaning of philosophy and cannot hope to describe the complex activity which philosophy is. In fact, if one focuses on the kind of activities philosophers engage in, it is easier to understand what philosophy is. What, then, do philosophers do when they philosophize? The answer is that they ask, and try in various ways to answer, three sorts of questions: (1) What do you mean? (Or, what does *it* — the word, the concept — mean?) (2) How do you know? (Or, what, in general constitute the grounds or kinds of grounds for claiming to know something?) (3) What is presupposed? (Or, what assumptions or presuppositions are you now making or must you make for the proposition you are now asserting?) It is when one acquires the habit of asking these questions about one's own and others' speech and writings that one begins to be a philosopher. As you acquire the habit of asking (and also answering) these sorts of questions in the context of education you will be on your way to becoming a philosopher of education.

Lest you think this habit of mind is easily acquired and does not require effort and practice, it is well for us to dwell on each of these questions in turn to see just what is involved.

Three Philosophical Questions

What do you mean?
When a philosopher asks, 'What do you mean?' he is not so much

enquiring into what *you* as an individual mean by a term, but into the meaning of the words you are using, or more accurately the concepts for which the words you are using are the labels. It is therefore a conceptual, not merely a verbal, inquiry. The question is equivalent to 'What is an X?', where X is the concept (or word) under scrutiny and the 'is' is one of identity, not predication. This last distinction between two kinds of uses for 'is' should be clearly kept in mind because it is one of the ways in which philosophical activity (and a philosophical statement) is identified. When we say, 'A bachelor is an unmarried adult male', the words following the 'is' are (perhaps, see below) collectively identical to the meaning of the term 'bachelor'. Thus we can speak of the 'is' of identity. When we say such things as, 'A bachelor is unlikely to have children', we are predicating things (giving some additional information) about bachelors. This can be called the 'is' of predication. Often it is difficult to say which 'is' is being employed. (Consider, for example, 'Peace is disarming'.) But it is the mark of a good philosopher to be able to sort this out. One way he proceeds is by attempting to provide the necessary *and* sufficient (jointly sufficient) conditions for calling something an X. This is not an easy thing to do with concepts that puzzle us and are in need of philosophical inquiry. Even for concepts that do not puzzle us, it is not easy to do. Where the X stands for 'bachelor', consider the following:

A bachelor is   (a)   unmarried.
                   (b)   happy.
                   (c)   female.
                   (d)   male.
                   (e)   adult.

Are conditions (a) to (e) jointly sufficient, that is, both necessary and sufficient for calling someone a bachelor? Clearly (b) is predication and therefore does not belong in this series where the 'is' in the statement is one of identity. Some women have suggested that (c) should be included because of the negative connotation surrounding 'spinster', the female equivalent of bachelor. But of course this would amount to legislating a new use for the term, which has problems of its own (see below, *Programmatic definitions*). An accurate analysis would have to exclude (c). Conditions (a), (d), and (e) are clearly necessary; but are they sufficient? One could argue that they are not. A divorced man is not usually called a 'bachelor', though he is unmarried, adult, and male. So one would probably want to include another condition such as 'never married'.

Others have suggested that 'homo sapiens' should be a condition, since bachelor is a term reserved for human beings. So even with very non-puzzling easy concepts the task is difficult to complete accurately. That is because so many of the concepts we use are not that precise. And the less precise, the more puzzling, and the more profound and complex the concept, the more in need of philosophical scrutiny they are likely to be. So perhaps, as Hirst and Peters observe[3], one may not always be successful in finding and specifying *all* the necessary conditions for difficult concepts. We may have to be satisfied with pin-pointing only *some* necessary conditions, *i.e.*, with a *weak* sense of definition. The reason for this is not only that language changes (as social life itself changes), but also that certain words have never been used very precisely in speech in general. The provision of necessary and sufficient conditions for the use of words is then only an ideal. It is the ideal philosophers strive for as they attempt to find the principles or rules that govern the use of words in a living public language. This is what philosophers are after when they ask 'What do you mean?' The importance of this task is difficult to over-emphasize. Many impatient, practically-minded educationalists have been critical of the analytic task of philosophy of education, arguing that philosophers 'fiddle' with words while the educational 'Rome' burns. The criticism is misplaced. Educational language is full of jargon and educational literature replete with inherently difficult concepts. Added to this is careless use and misuse of ordinary terms, all of which warrants a great deal of philosophical attention. In fact one is tempted to say that failure to convey meaning is one of the major problems in educational discourse and causes much unnecessary confusion, lack of progress in educational research, and even animosity and distrust. Philosophy can be of great help in avoiding these. Yet despite this important function of philosophy in dealing with the problem of meaning, that is only one important first task of philosophy. Philosophers are also concerned with questions of truth and knowledge, but only after questions of meaning have been settled. Questions of meaning are always logically prior to questions of truth. But once meaning is clear, philosophers ask 'How do you know?'

How do you know?

Not all 'How do you know?' questions are of a philosophical kind. If in response to the statement 'Smoking causes cancer' you ask 'How do you know?' all that is required is for the speaker to cite the appropriate evidence. There is very little philosophical interest in such remarks. But suppose someone answers: 'Because a lot of people say so'. Now the philosopher might well remark that that is not the appropriate kind of evidence. No matter how many people believe something to be true, that could not constitute the reason or grounds for it to be true. Mere believing is just not the sort of thing that constitutes the grounds (or the evidence) for anything. It is not in the right type of category. Philosophers, that is to say, are not so much interested in a particular claim to knowledge but about a class of claims, about the general sorts of grounds for supporting various types of statements. They ask and try to answer questions like: What sort of statement is this? Is it historical? empirical? logical? aesthetic? moral? And once it is known what type of statement is made, philosophers ask after the appropriate evidence for that type of statement.

Sometimes a statement by itself has little interest for a philosopher, but a great deal of interest in context with other statements. Thus a philosopher may observe that a series of statements does not lead to an alleged conclusion, perhaps because premises are missing or a derivation is not allowed according to the rules of logic. Philosophy in fact is very much concerned with the rules of logic and various kinds of errors in logical argument. Philosophers typically point out such thinking errors as: contradiction, inconsistency, *ad hominem* attacks, circularity, incompleteness, category mistakes, and so on. Philosophers, in other words, are very much concerned with argument and assessment of argument.

At other times they are interested in singular statements when such statements are themselves puzzling because of the unusual nature of their claim. (Actually, any and every statement *can* have philosophical dimensions, since all statements have meaning and function, and reflect thought about which there can be second-order thought and discussion.) It is not always clear when first looking at a statement what sort of evidence is needed for sufficiently grounding, or legitimately satisfying the demands for the right to be claiming, a particular statement. Consider, for example, the following statement: Children ought not to be punished because it interferes with their moral education. It is not at all obvious without some philosophical reflection whether the 'ought' is hypothetical/scientific or moral/prescriptive or even whether the claim is true by definition. If it is to be taken scientifically, then it would be necessary for the speaker to cite the empirical evidence showing that if children are punished then they do not become morally educated.

The speaker, however, might be claiming that for moral reasons children ought not to be punished whatever the consequences about their further learning. It would then be a moral proposition requiring outside support for the moral position taken. The speaker could even be construed as intending to claim that whatever children learn by being punished it does not count as moral education. This would be making a claim about the meaning of moral education and hence a truth by definition. Reflection on the sentence reveals that the speaker is making a relatively straightforward empirical claim. But the sentence invites philosophical reflection in a most representative way. It opens up questioning which is typically philosophical and illustrates how the three questions, What do you mean? How do you know? and What is presupposed? all run together and coincide around a single claim. Whether the claim is true or not depends in part on the meaning of 'punishment', 'moral', and 'education'. If we take 'education' to mean *at least* the acquisition of knowledge and understanding (and later in the book we shall see that central uses of the term require that condition) then if moral *education* (as distinct from training) is possible at all it must be because there are certain moral truths which are knowable; and so the proposition implies a certain view of, or meaning for, the term 'morality', namely, that morality is more than just an attitude or a matter of long-term preferences one is committed to. One who believes that education is just a matter of training, and morality merely personal commitments, might well take a different view about the truth of the proposition under discussion than one who takes a different position on the meaning of those terms. In other words the philosophical concern with meaning turns out to be equally and at the same time concern for the truth of the proposition and how the truth of the statement is to be arrived at. But more. There is also simultaneously concern with assumptions.

What is presupposed?
The statement, 'Children ought not to be punished because it interferes with their moral education', also raises questions about assumptions or presuppositions, as already noted. The speaker is assuming that moral education of some form is possible. Now of course, every speaker always makes certain assumptions about meanings of words and conditions in the world. When I say, 'Please fetch me some water', I am assuming a number of things: that you understand my words; that there is water available; that you are able to fetch some, and so on. But not always is it necessary to examine

these assumptions; nor is it always a philosophical activity to do so. Only when the truth of propositions comes into question or the meaning of the terms are indeed puzzling and in need of clarification does the examination of assumptions made amount to philosophical activity. Thus in the above statement, if it is clear that the speaker has a concept of education (in the 'knowledge and understanding' sense), then it is a matter of logic that he *must* assume a certain characterization of morality such that moral knowledge and understanding is possible. Otherwise what the speaker says doesn't make sense. So when a philosopher begins to think about what has been said at the second-order level, then what seemed like a straightforward empirical statement turns out to be a highly controversial but also quite complex and profound issue. Indeed, one of the most important, difficult, and profound books in moral philosophy ever written (I. Kant's *Fundamental Principles of the Metaphysics of Morals*) was an attempt to make explicit what is presupposed in making sense of moral language and action. Similarly, R.S. Peters' book *Ethics and Education* is an examination of ethical issues in education and an attempt to seek justification for the ethical principles involved by 'probing behind them in order to make explicit what they implicitly presuppose'.[4] This is an extremely difficult activity and is definitely at a second-order if not third-order level. It illustrates what should by now have become obvious — that philosophy is a multi-faceted and diverse activity. It is very difficult to state precisely what it is. The above has been an attempt to shed some light on the nature of the activity by discussing the three sorts of questions philosophers are typically concerned with.

Definitions and the Problem of Meaning

We have seen that philosophy is typically concerned with meaning, with justification, and with examination of assumptions. We have also seen that the latter two are often dependent on the first or that the problems of justification for the truth of propositions and problems about assumptions made are dissolved once the problem of meaning is adequately addressed. It is for this reason that some philosophers think (understandably, though mistakenly) that the task of the philosopher is entirely that of conceptual analysis and the clarification of meaning. We now know that is not quite so. But the task of conceptual analysis is still one of the major concerns of philosophers and is particularly important in education. In any case it is with the problem of meaning that the remainder of this chapter is concerned; and it is concerned with it in a technical sense. That is, we will not be discussing the meaning of educationally important terms such as 'teaching', 'learning', and 'creativity' just yet; but we want to examine further why philosophy is required for this task rather than just consulting a dictionary.

Defining and the Philosophical Search for Meaning

Beginning students of philosophy (and philosophers of education) often ask why the problem of meaning in educational (or any other) discourse cannot simply be solved by consulting a dictionary. Part of the problem it must be noted, can be solved by a dictionary. If we want to know how some words are used we can consult a good dictionary and discover there a list of the complete set of conditions describing the rules for the use of a term. See, for example, any good dictionary for the definition of the word 'triangle'. But it should also be noted that for such terms there is no need for philosophical reflection and analysis. It is only when the meaning of terms in the public language are not clear and precise that the philosophical task comes into play. But for such terms the dictionary can do no better than accurately reflect the confusion surrounding the term as ordinarily used. Even then it can do that only in a brief, summary form, often using terms that are no less clear than the term being defined. What does it help to say that 'fairness' is 'moral equality' when both terms are equally difficult to grasp? A dictionary then, when it attempts to render clear the meaning of those terms giving rise to wonder and puzzlement in ordinary speech, is at best a crude instrument attempting to reflect in an extremely abbreviated form the way in which an unreflecting public uses terms in ordinary language even when the usage is inconsistent, conceptually crude, or confusing.

By contrast a philosopher will attempt to render clear, perhaps for the first time, the precise meaning of a term by making explicit the rules for the use of a term and in detail describe how the term functions in context with other terms. Philosophers pay close attention to how terms are used in discussion and argument. Philosophy thus becomes a much richer activity than merely noting some necessary and sufficient conditions in defining terms. At the same time the results of philosophical work often are reflected in more accurate and more meaningful speech and later recorded in dictionary definitions. Sometimes philosophical statements (for example, punishment involves the infliction of pain or unpleasantness by an authority on one who has violated a rule) look very much like definitions or partial definitions. But that is so only if the definitions referred to are of a particular type, namely, those which report standard public usage. There are other kinds of definitions whose function is very different. In order to see more clearly how and why philosophy is necessary, and to be more alert about how language in general and definitions in particular can bewitch our intelligence, it is important to observe how various kinds of definitions serve different purposes.

Definitions and their Uses

When speakers (or writers) fail to communicate and are invited to define their terms, they usually recommence by providing the hearer (or reader) with a definition of some sort; but by no means do they necessarily always do the same things. Three different writers can be engaged in three very different activities, though each of them is 'defining his terms'. Thanks to such writers as I. Scheffler[5] and R.G. Olson[6] we now have a very good idea of how importantly and distinctly different are the activities of providing a reader with three distinct types of definitions — stipulative definitions, reportive definitions, and programmatic definitions.

Stipulative definitions

Stipulative definitions are used by writers (and *mutatis mutandis* for speakers) to indicate how they as individuals are going to use a particular term in a given context, space, period of time, or purpose. The term defined may be one never before used in the language (Scheffler's 'inventive' stipulation) or one that has been used before (Scheffler's 'non-inventive' stipulation). Even if the term has been used before (e.g., 'chalk') there is no necessity for the definition either in whole or in part to reflect what the word ordinarily means. The function of a stipulative definition is to reveal the writer's intention for the given context; and it is strictly a private affair. It should be made clear that people can and do sometimes make ordinary terms mean very strange things and very different things from what is ordinarily understood by them. Thus I can stipulate, for purposes of illustration, that in the next few sentences I will use the term 'chalk' to mean 'a small roll of finely cut tobacco wrapped in thin paper for smoking'. Now I can freely say that some people damage their health by lighting up their chalks. It is pointless to try to stop me from giving 'chalk' this meaning. A point we learnt from

Alice (in ... *Wonderland*) is that we are masters of words; not words our masters. Nor is it correct to say that I would not be telling the truth in asserting that smoking chalks is hazardous to health. Truth or falsity is not a feature of how stipulative definitions are assessed. They are assessed rather on grounds of their utility in accomplishing the purposes of the writer — do they provide a handy label for a difficult idea? do they provide the necessary abbreviatory function for complex notions? do they facilitate ease of grasping and remembering the meaning assigned? and so on. However — and this needs underlining — had I as the writer not gone on notice that I was stipulating, then the charge of dishonesty might well have been appropriate. If without notice and explanation I tell a small child that inhaling chalk impurities causes cancer I might well be accused of telling him a lie. Writers who stipulate therefore almost always go on notice by use of phrases such as 'I will take X to mean that ... '; 'For the duration of this speech I will refer to X as ... '; 'I will use the term X to refer to ... '; or 'X, in the sense in which I mean it, is ... '; and so on. When people do not thus announce a stipulation, it is usually understood that they are using a definition of another kind, almost always a reportive kind.

Reportive definitions

Unlike stipulative definitions, reportive definitions do intend to report accurately prior usage. Scheffler[7] calls these 'descriptive' definitions, since they purport to describe how a term is used in ordinary public speech. Truth or falsity is very much a feature of these definitions. Descriptive definitions are assessed according to how well they do accurately embody given conventions of usage. They are not arbitrary as stipulations are arbitrary. However, the fact that concepts have a public life and words labelling them have a convention in usage (otherwise communication would become impossible), it does not follow that words cannot change in meaning or that concepts are frozen in a language. A view about language which holds that there are clear and important conventions in how words (and concepts) function does not need to subscribe to the further view of 'essentialism' in meaning, which holds that there are essences in nature which words mirror. The fact that sometimes conventions of usage change merely means that dictionaries from time to time need rewriting. It also means that philosophy's task is never done. For when philosophers attempt to lay bare the rules for the meaning of words, they are not looking for rules assigned by individuals to certain words, as in stipulations, but are attempting to ferret out public conventions and extant distinctions in the language. As such they do descriptive conceptual analysis. When philosophers do make explicit the rules for the use of words, and as a result of this those who are illuminated by the analysis use words more carefully by eliminating pre-analysis inaccuracies and inconsistencies, they are in a small way contributing to the shift in conventional usage. In this way hazy distinctions and nascent concepts already in the language are made more clear and precise. But this activity is very different from that of some devotees of certain programs and policies who legislate changes in language through the use of 'legislative' or 'programmatic' definitions.

Programmatic definitions

Sometimes people who favour certain courses of action but cannot or do not want to support that action or policy with good reasons and appropriate evidence attempt to effect a change in speech and action by legislating a shift in the meaning of words. For them language manipulation is a substitute for good argument. What happens is something like the scenario that follows. A speaker, knowing that a hearer in general terms shares his attitude toward a particular subject under discussion, say, education, will then attempt to secure the hearer's support for a particular controversial policy or programme in education by giving the hearer a definition in which the program is buried or written in. Usually the speaker will begin by emphasizing that, 'The *real* meaning of education is . . .' or 'Quite obviously at the heart of education is . . .' and then comes the definition which includes the program. Notice, for example, the difference in the policy, program, or prescription in the following two programmatic definitions: (1) 'The real meaning of education is self-actualization through growth in knowledge and understanding of the self'; and (2) 'Education can genuinely be so called only when it involves knowledge and understanding that leads to social responsibility and well-being'. The definitions, it will be noted, do not depart entirely from reportive definitions; if they did, they would not be accepted and thus the program would not be advanced. Usually the definitions either add unnecessary conditions or delete necessary ones. In that way they appear respectable to the unaware and so does the program thus advanced. They raise moral or practical issues which have not been argued. The attempt illegitimately to win a case by definition is one way in which programmatic definitions function. It has also been argued, by Scheffler for example, that sometimes it is quite legitimate to use programmatic definitions when (1) the arguments for a program in a definition have been made and are acceptable, and (2) when an analysis of pre-definitional use indicates that ordinary usage is vague with respect to necessary and sufficient conditions. In such cases there does not in fact seem to be a settled use for a particular term. The philosopher's role in these situations is to specify in which several ways a term functions, to try to unearth the assumptions being made in each of the several possible uses, and to attempt to show what kinds of definitions are being used in any given context. In laying bare the logical grammar of words employed in language, he attempts to note where arguments are required, what kinds of arguments are appropriate, and to isolate the principles upon which arguments rest and decisions are made. He helps to free the understanding in order to assist intelligent and rational decision-making. The philosopher can thus help in the ever-growing problem of trying to make sense of educational language and, more importantly, thereby enable better judgment and better practice in education itself.

Recommended further readings:

Hirst, P.H. and Peters, R.S. (1970) *The Logic of Education*, Routledge and Kegan Paul, pp. 1–16.
Olson, R.G. (1969) *Meaning and Argument*, Harcourt, Brace and World Inc., Chapters 2, 3, 6, & 7.
Scheffler, I. (1960) *The Language of Education*, Springfield, Illinois, Charles C. Thomas, pp. 3–35.

Notes

1   Bigge, M.L. (1982) *Educational Philosophies for Teachers*, Charles E. Merrill Publ. Co.
2   Hirst, P.H. (1974) *Knowledge and the Curriculum*, Routledge and Kegan Paul, pp. 1–2.
3   Hirst, P.H. and Peters, R.S. (1970) *The Logic of Education*, Routledge and Kegan Paul, p.6.
4   Peters, R.S. (1966) *Ethics and Education*, George Allen and Unwin, London, p.114.
5   Scheffler, I. (1960) *The Language of Education*, Charles C. Thomas, Springfield Illinois.
6   Olson, R.G. (1969) *Meaning and Argument*, Harcourt, Brace and World Inc.
7   Scheffler, I. (1960) *op. cit.*, Chapter 1.

Questions and Exercises

Answer each question below as briefly as possible:
1   What is a concept?
2   How do philosophers go about clarifying concepts? (In your response give an example and show why a good dictionary cannot replace a good philosopher.)
3   Besides clarifying concepts, what is philosophy concerned with? (Again, give an example.)
4   Explain why the ability to use a word appropriately is not a necessary condition for possession of a concept although it may be a sufficient condition.
5   Which of the following sentences are philosophical? Explain why you think they are or are not.

(a)   Teaching requires at least an act of display, or indication, of subject matter.
(b)   For teaching to be effective it is necessary to be clear about objectives, to allow room for discussion, and above all to be engaging.
(c)   Because teaching is over-demanding, underpaid, and poorly appreciated by the public many teachers leave the profession even though it can be and ought to be one of the most rewarding professions of all.

Answer the following questions in a sentence or two:
1   What purposes are served by stipulative definitions?
2   What criteria must a good reportive (or descriptive) definition satisfy?
3   What is an alternative and presumably better way of instituting a new and better policy in education than by the use of programmatic (legislative) definitions?
4   How would you be able to determine whether a speaker is using a programmatic definition rather than an unsuccessful reportive definition?

Each of the sentences below is one of the following:
(a)   a descriptive (reportive) definition
(b)   a stipulative definition
(c)   a programmatic (legislative) definition
(d)   an empirically verifiable statement
(e)   an evaluative (or moral) statement
(f)   a slogan

Indicate which they are by placing the appropriate letter, (a) to (f) in the bracket in front of each sentence.

( )   'Education, in the sense in which I mean it, may be defined as the formation, by means of instruction, of certain mental habits and a certain outlook on life and the world.' B. Russell, *Mysticism and Logic*, Allen and Unwin, 1971, p. 37.

( ) 'Job qualifications for entry into nearly all occupations include an increasingly high and specified level of formal schooling.' James E. McClellan, *Toward an Effective Critique of American Education*, J.B. Lippincott, 1968, pp. 19.

( ) Education is the systematic assimilation of society's new-born members into the existing culture.

( ) 'According to the norm of universal citizenship, everyone has ... a right to education.' — J. McClellan, 1968, *op. cit.*, p. 51.

( ) In its widest sense, teaching is an intentional act designed to bring about learning.

( ) 'To teach, in the standard sense, is at some points at least to submit oneself to the understanding and independent judgment of the pupil, to his demand for reasons, to his sense of what constitutes an adequate explanation.' I. Scheffler, *The Language of Education*, 1960, p. 57.

( ) A school is a place or institution designed to further pupils' training or education through teaching and learning.

( ) Education is a time-consuming and difficult enterprise.

( ) Education is for life; and life is for education.

( ) Education, properly conceived, is assisting the child in developing his potential.

( ) 'It is well to say every now and then that grading ought to be abandoned.' P. Goodman, quoted in J. McClellan, 1968, *op. cit.*, p. 281

( ) Punishment is the intentional infliction of pain by an authority on an offender for a breach of some rule.

( ) A word is a verbal symbol labelling a concept and used in speech or writing to communicate meaning.

( ) Children must never be forced to learn.

( ) 'In-service training is the cheapest, quickest and most effective way to train people in industry.' J.D. Wilson in *The Best of Times; the Worst of Times*, Holt, Rinehart, and Winston, 1972, p. 277.

CHAPTER 2

Metaphors in Educational Discourse

Pitfalls of Language — Vagueness, Ambiguity, Emotive Uses

In this chapter we want to examine certain inherent characteristics of our language which can become obstacles to clear thinking and rational argument in education. We have already observed from our study into the nature of philosophy in Chapter I how philosophers place great importance on language. Enquiry into words and meanings is an important philosophical activity because there is an important logical connection between language and thinking. Language can in fact be viewed as a tool for thinking because words label concepts and thinking presupposes the possession of concepts; we think with concepts. Our thoughts, then, will be as clear or as clouded as the words and sentences which are used to express these thoughts. If communication is to improve and clarity in thought and argument to prevail, it is important for us to be aware of certain features of language and on guard against certain pitfalls that prevent this from happening. Vagueness and ambiguity are two characteristics of language that can become pitfalls or traps and contribute to unclear thinking and generally to a breakdown in communication.

A term is vague when there is no answer to the question of whether a term applies in a specific case and further when there is not even the possibility of knowing whether it applies. In other words, the difficulty is not in our lack of knowledge, but in the term itself. There can thus be vagueness of degree, since there is no agreement on the necessary and sufficient conditions for the use of the term (e.g., 'fruit'); or there can be vagueness of number, where no cut-off point is agreed upon (e.g., 'middle-aged'). Removal of vagueness is not always possible or desirable. A wise communicator will use the extent of precision required for his purposes.

Ambiguity is concerned with multiple (usually double) meanings. In these cases two (or more) meanings are clear and specific (and hence not vague) but it is not clear which meaning is referred to. A speaker or writer uses language ambiguously when he does not in the context make clear which of several possible uses he is referring to. Thus 'normal' could refer to either a neutral *description* of what is done or to an *evaluation* of what is morally permissible. This is an instance of semantic ambiguity. An example of syntactical ambiguity is, 'The police force was ordered to stop the drinking', where the double meaning results from the faulty sentence structure. Ambiguities are avoidable and interfere with communication.

Another kind of trap one should be aware of is emotive use of language, occurring when certain word choices by a writer tend to deceive the reader by eliciting from him an evaluation of a phenomenon to coincide with the writer's own under the guise of a neutral description. The evaluations of the speaker are clearly evident in: 'stone-age mentality', 'abortion, the merciless slaughter of the innocent', 'our courageous and honourable leader'. There is little point in trying to legislate emotive usages out of existence. In fact they can be desirable in many circumstances. But there is a great deal of point in being aware of what is going on when they are being used.

Another form of language use which may prevent clear thought and cause problems in communication is the use of metaphor. Educational language is replete with metaphor, as is true in all ordinary language. Metaphors can be very useful for purposes of illuminating difficult ideas or notions. They can also be very misleading if not carefully employed. Because metaphors are so prevalent in educational language, helping clarity of thought but also very misleading at times, the remainder of this chapter will be devoted to a discussion of how generally metaphors function and how they can be assessed, followed by detailed discussion of several important educational metaphors.

Metaphorical Language

A metaphorical statement draws an important analogy between two things, one of which is well known, the other not so well known. The intent of the user of the metaphor is to shed light on (notice, that too is a metaphor) or explain to the listener/reader the nature of the unknown thing by juxtaposing the two things (actually or in imagination) with the use of terms such as 'like' (My love is like a red, red rose) or 'is' (Education is growth), but not saying exactly what the likeness consists in. How is my love like a red rose? In color? smell? shape? texture? Surely none of these. But what then? Well, that is where the assessment of the analogy comes in. I Scheffler, in his illuminating chapter on metaphors in *The Language of Education* writes: 'If a given metaphorical statement is to be judged worthwhile or apt, the analogy suggested must be important with respect to criteria relevant to the context of the utterance'.[1] In other words we look for aptness, suitability, appropriateness of the comparison in significant ways. Where this is not the case, the metaphor can in fact mislead and cloud our thinking about the unknown subject rather than illuminate it. However, one must not give up the search for fruitful comparisons too soon. My love may not be like a rose in those respects so far suggested, but may be like Burns' image of perfection, evoking feelings both sensuous and aesthetic. So if you wish to assess a metaphor for its utility in conveying meaning, one way would be to make a list of all those characteristics which you think are apt in the analogy and another list of those you think are inapt.

Analyzing Educational Metaphors

The Growth Metaphor

The molding and art metaphors with connotations of shaping the child have had extended influence on the thinking about education for many centuries. More recently, particularly in this century, the growth metaphor has had a significant influence on educational thought, connected as it is with the so-called 'progressive' movement in education. The metaphor continues to hold sway in contemporary times. Such notions as 'fulfilling the potentials of each child', 'individualized instruction appropriate to the uniqueness of each child', 'education to meet the needs of each child', 'children should be self-directed', 'education as self-realization, self-fulfilment, self-actualization' — these and many more educational ideas and practices find their theoretical source in the growth model. The growth concept has, in other words, become central in educational thinking. According to R.F. Dearden it functions 'as a symbolic image, pregnant with meaning and rich in emotional appeals'.[2] Indeed, it is sometimes said that education is growth, almost as though that is the definition of education. John Dewey says 'Education means the enterprise of supplying the conditions which ensure growth.... The criterion of the value of school education is the extent in which it creates a desire for continued growth and supplies the means for making the desire effective in fact'.[3] With the obvious appeal the growth metaphor has, it would be very surprising if there were not some aspects of education that are illuminated by use of the growth analogy. These will be pointed out below. But a good metaphor is not always good in every context.[4] And so a careful analysis and assessment of the use of the metaphor reveals a number of disanalogies or faulty comparisons. Thus a good case could be made for the view that the growth metaphor is overall misleading and has done considerable harm in educational thought and practice. But, to repeat a point, this is not a matter of black and white but a matter of isolating specific strengths and weaknesses in the analogy.

Aptness of the growth metaphor

Dewey surely was correct in two respects in using the growth metaphor to depict education. First, education, like growth, is on-going and continuous, or at least ideally it should be. Unlike the potter and chiseler who cease work when the product is 'finished', in education the learning continues to life's end and without surcease. The educational process, Dewey says, is one of continual reorganization, reconstruction, and transformation. There is no point at which one can say, 'I am now fully educated', anymore than one can say that a tree has reached maturity and stops growing, unless it is dead.

Secondly, the growth metaphor hints at rather than more directly expresses the view that education has intrinsic value. This point about education is forcefully made by R.S. Peters, as we shall later see. It was also part of Dewey's view about education. He says: 'The educational process has no end beyond itself; it is its own end. There is nothing to which growth is relative save more growth; there is nothing to which education is subordinate save more education'.[5]

Another feature of the growth model, mentioned neither by Scheffler nor Dewey, is that with respect to teaching it is perhaps detrimental to a child to force intellectual development just as it may be damaging to a plant to force open a bloom. The aptness of this observation will depend to a considerable extent on whether or not one subscribes to the very notion of intellectual development itself, where 'development' is itself a metaphor.[6]

In any case just because these few aspects of the growth model are apt and illuminating about education, it does not follow that other aspects are. Indeed, taking Scheffler's lead, we can quite forcefully argue that Dewey and his followers and many contemporary thinkers decidedly have gone astray by pushing the metaphor too far.

Inaptness of the growth metaphor

In a number of respects the growth metaphor misleads rather than enlightens. Some of the problems with the metaphor noted below are discussed fully by Scheffler and will be alluded to here only in summary form; others not mentioned by Scheffler will be more fully discussed.

First, as Scheffler clearly points out, the metaphor falsely parallels physical growth with intellectual, social, and moral growth. Secondly, the metaphor wrongly suggests that the value judgment in education can be avoided by taking a more 'scientific' look at children to see what their potential is and then develop it. But, of course, not all of a child's potential *can* be fulfilled; for some directions of growth are mutually exclusive. One cannot become both a Marquis de Sade *and* a St. Francis. Furthermore, some potential *should* not be fulfilled. Perhaps all of us have the potential to be rogues, but that is no reason to develop that potential. We shall later see, in discussing the work of R.S. Peters in Chapter 3, that the value judgment in education is unavoidable.

Thirdly, there is in the analogy a unwarranted reliance on highly questionable assumptions about human nature. The assumption is that children as a group have, and that each individual child has, a quite firmly fixed nature from birth (or even prior to) which more or less determines our mature state if only that nature is allowed to flourish unimpeded. It is almost as if there exists in our genes certain dictates with respect to our educational development which guide that development to a natural given outcome. In other words in the age-old debate about nurture versus nature, the growth theorists have come out too strongly on the side of nature, ignoring the evidence of nurture, of the importance of child-rearing and the influence of education on the child's development. Moreover, they take a very benign view of human nature; that is, they almost always deny that anything perverse such as over-acquisitiveness or selfishness is part of human nature. They believe very much in the 'noble savage' rather than in 'original sin'. Later in the book we will briefly examine some views on human nature. For now it needs only to be noted that growth theorists tend to take a very one-sided view of human nature against what seems to be fairly solid evidence to the contrary. But let us suppose that we *do* have a fixed nature much as the growth theorists suggest. Would that be a reason to encourage such development? Suppose it were discovered that we have a very acquisitive tendency by nature, why would that constitute a reason for one to enhance and satisfy that nature and even build an 'educational' program to fit? It wouldn't. And this takes us to a final knock-out argument against the growth theorists.

The subscribers to the growth metaphor in education tend to commit what is known as the 'naturalistic fallacy'. By this is meant, as almost any good introduction to Ethics or Morals will tell you, that one wrongly and without warrant derives an 'ought' statement from an 'is' statement. In the growth model it is wrongly thought that whatever *is* the case with respect to the nature of children or of a particular child has implications for what *ought* to be done to the child to help it conform with nature. And that is simply a mistake in logic. Since this error recurs again and again in educational discourse it is instructive here to elaborate somewhat. It is a requirement of deductive logic that no more can be allowed in a conclusion than is contained in the premises. In the case of the naturalistic fallacy the 'ought' in the conclusion is not contained in the premises; hence the error. David Hume put it as follows:

> In every system of morality which I have hitherto met with, I have always remarked that the author proceeds for some time in the ordinary way of reasoning . . . or makes observations concerning human affairs; when, of a sudden I am surprised to find, that instead of the usual copulation of propositions, *is*, and *is not*, I meet with no proposition that is not connected with an *ought* or *ought not*. This change is imperceptible; but is however of the last consequence. For as this *ought or ought not* expresses some new relation or affirmation, it is necessary that it should be observed and explained; and at the same time a reason should be given for what seems altogether inconceivable, how this new relation can be a deduction from others, which are entirely different from it.[7]

What Hume was looking for was the 'ought' in the premises from which the ought in the conclusion could logically follow. From an 'is' *alone* nothing logically follows. Thus, from the sentence 'Children like to play' it does not follow that 'they ought to be taught the play way', though it is tempting for some people to argue precisely this way. However if we now add another premise, 'Children *ought* to be taught in the way they like it', then the conclusion does follow. But now one is not so tempted to accept the conclusion because one is not quite prepared to accept the required additional value premises containing the *ought*. Of course, there may be other reasons why children, perhaps, should be taught the 'play way', but reasons for that would need to be provided. The point is that simply because something *is* true, in this case that children like to play, nothing follows about what *ought* to be done. And likewise in the growth metaphor, simply because something *is* true in nature, nothing follows about how education *ought* to be conducted. To attempt to make that derivation is to commit the naturalistic fallacy.

We have seen, then, how the growth metaphor does not fare too well under analysis as an attempt to illuminate the concept of education. We shall now take a look at the 'organic' metaphor to see if it fares any better.

The Organic Metaphor

The 'organic' metaphor, as Scheffler calls it, or the cultural renewal model of education as an alternative articulaticn of it, is really an extension of the growth metaphor in some ways; but it does have significant differences and important separate issues which warrant separate discussion.

In the organic metaphor it is an organism rather than a plant, as in the growth metaphor, that is likened to education. According to the organic metaphor, education is the process of cultural renewal and continuity. This process is similar to the process of cell replacement and environmental adaptation of an organism to ensure its survival and continuity.[8]

In assessing the appropriateness of this model Scheffler fairly fully and accurately explores the weakness of the model. He is less explicit about any strengths that the analogy suggests.

Aptness of the organic metaphor

First, it can fairly safely be said that education is at least partly cultural renewal. It transmits (cannot but transmit) elements of a culture. That does not mean that education and socialization (where that term is roughly equivalent to acculturation) are synonymous. Far from it. Successful socialization *can* result in very poor and limited education; and very good education *can* be socially very disruptive. Perfect symmetry between education and socialization occurs only when a perfectly educated society is completely successful in transmitting its culture, an ideal that is rarely, if ever, achieved. Nonetheless, when a society deliberately goes about to transmit what they feel is 'the best that has been thought and said'[9] then it is performing its function of conserving an element of the culture with the view to renewal and continuity.

Secondly, the organic model does hint at the suggestion that education does indeed contribute to the health and well-being of a society, particularly an open society which values knowledge and understanding. It would be very surprising if an educated person, one who has knowledge and understanding in breadth and depth, were not able to do something useful and valuable and contribute to the society as a whole. The metaphor helps to highlight this point; though, of couse, as Scheffler notes, what constitutes health in a society is not specifiable independent of what is socially desirable.

Inaptness of the organic metaphor
When one also considers the weaknesses of the organic metaphor it becomes quite evident that the metaphor does not serve very well to illuminate education. The metaphor is flawed in serious ways.

First, the analogy in the metaphor falsely relies on a human development theory in which biological regeneration, following relatively invariant physical laws, is thought to be similar to cultural regeneration, which does not follow fixed rules or laws. Rather, a society makes value judgments about what constitutes its own health and well-being. Terms such as 'working', 'properly functioning', 'problem free', 'coping', and so on, used to express a society which is in a state of 'health', are parasitic on value judgments regarding how societies ought to be. They are not neutral descriptions about conditions of mere survival, but judgments about quality of survival.

Secondly, and in elaboration of the above, biological development and improvement presupposes clear and specific criteria for health and well-being of the organism. An organism's blood pressure and pulse, for example, must be within a certain range for the organism to function normally. There are no such criteria for 'normal function' to determine the health of a society. These criteria are based on alternative choices in society. Social and moral decisions are crucial and deliberation necessary for making 'adjustments' in the social order.

There is too the point made by Scheffler regarding the importance of the manner of cultural transmission in education. In biological renewal the manner of renewal is not significant. In cultural renewal which disregards education, the manner of transmitting the culture is disregarded. Methods of threat, conditioning, or indoctrination might be acceptable. But not so in education. As we shall see more clearly later, there is an important procedural criterion for education which is not required for mere socialization into a culture.

Finally, we can mention again the temptation on the part of those who use the organic metaphor to commit the naturalistic fallacy. The temptation is to think that because something *is* extant in the cultures it *ought* to be transmitted. Often we hear arguments to the effect that if a certain practice — say, the use of computers — *is* widespread in society that we therefore *ought* to make children computer literate. (There might very well be good reasons why children should become computer literate, but the reason that computers are everywhere available is not the justification for that.) No mere description of what are the elements of a culture can constitute a reason why that element should be perpetuated and improved upon. For the latter, independent judgments of value need to be made.

We have seen then that the organic metaphor, like the other metaphors we have discussed, does not help very much in illuminating the nature of education. Indeed, as for the growth metaphor, the organic metaphor, when assessed for its strengths and weaknesses, can be seen as more misleading than illuminating about education.

The point of examining these metaphors is not that we should not use metaphors at all; but rather that we should be more aware of when and how metaphors are used and then be in a position to assess how useful they are. It is doubtful, as some would argue, that we could in the interest of pristine clarity and precision, delete from educational language the use of metaphor altogether. H. Entwistle, for example, says, 'It is arguable that our educational theories would become sharper instruments, less liable to fallacy, if we could dispense with metaphors altogether'.[10] It is also doubtful that, 'from the point of view of the theory of meaning, no clear distinction can be drawn between metaphorical and non-metaphorical uses of words'.[11] A reasonable position somewhere between these two extremes is D. Aspen's:

> Metaphors encapsulate and put forward proposals for another way of looking at things and of grasping inchoate intimations of possibilities, giving voice to meanings that are shifting, elusive, unstable, polymorphous, and illusory.[12]

Many educational concepts fit the description as shifting, elusive, and polymorphous; and so we can expect that metaphors will and should continue to be used in educational discourse. We should be cautious, though, against letting certain metaphors become mindless slogans and 'thought stoppers' because of orthodoxy and dogmatism that builds around them. And it is precisely when such orthodoxy builds around certain metaphors that initial insights get lost, analogies are pushed too far, and the overall effect of the use of the metaphor becomes damagingly misleading. In the next chapter we shall see how the metaphor of 'education as initiation' as used by R.S. Peters can be misused by some who tend to orthodoxy, though the metaphor can provide considerable insight into the nature of education.

But before turning to that, it is important to remind ourselves that anyone who is concerned with and about education should be familiar with the above-noted features of language, not only in order to conduct one's own thinking in a careful and fruitful manner, but also in order to examine and evaluate other people's views, recommendations, or programmes in a rational and systematic way. Very often in educational discussions people will take refuge in and exploit these aspects of our language in an attempt to persuade, convince, or win over others to their programme. They try to gain acceptance of their views not by demonstrating the validity of their views through reasoned argument and citing of appropriate evidence, but by employing language that is vague, or ambiguous, or emotive, or metaphorical.

Recommended further readings:

SCHEFFLER, I. (1960) 'Educational metaphors' in *The Language of Education*, Springfield, Illinois, Charles C. Thomas, pp. 17–59.
HIRST, P.H. and PETERS, R.S. (1970) *The Logic of Education*, Routledge and Kegan Paul, pp. 42–59.
DEWEY, J. (1916) *Democracy and Education*, New York, Macmillan, ch. 4.

Notes

1 SCHEFFLER, I. (1960) *op. cit.*, p. 40.
2 See DEARDEN, R.F. (1968) *The Philosophy of Primary Education*, Routledge and Kegan Paul, London, p. 25.
3 DEWEY, J. (1916) *Democracy and Education*, Macmillan, New York, pp. 51, 53.
4 See SCHEFFLER, I. (1960) *op. cit.*, p. 52.
5 DEWEY, J. (1916) *op. cit.*, pp. 50, 51.

6   See below, 'Inaptness of the organic metaphor' for further discussion.
7   HUME, D. *Treatise on Human Nature*, Bk. III, Part I, Section 2.
8   See SCHEFFLER, I. (1960) *op. cit.*, pp. 53–56.
9   The words are Matthew Arnold's.
10 ENTWISTLE, H. (1970) *Child-Centered Education*, Methuen, London, 1970, p. 156.
11 TAYLOR, D.M. (1970) *Explanation and Meaning*, University Press, Cambridge, p. 170.
12 In TAYLOR, W. (Ed.) (1984) *Metaphors of Education*, Institute of Education University of London, p. 34.

Questions and Exercises

As briefly as possible (two or three sentences) answer the following questions:
1   Is it possible and desirable to eliminate ambiguity in educational discourse? How about vagueness?
2   How do metaphors convey important information? How do they work?
3   Is it possible and desirable to eliminate metaphors from educational discourse?
4   What is the problem with attempts to develop all of the potentialities of every child?
5   In what sense are educators custodians of civilization? Should they be?
6   When, if ever, are education and socialization synonymous?
7   What sort of 'aims' of education rely on the socialization (organic) model of education?

In a paragraph or two answer the following questions:
1   'Education is growth'. Is this statement a definition? a metaphor? or an incidental observation about education? How illuminating is it to talk about education in this way?
2   How is education both like and unlike the process of cultural renewal?
3   What is the 'naturalistic fallacy'? Give examples of how it has caused mischief in educational discourse. Explain why it is important for educators to be aware of this fallacy
4   Briefly describe and discuss one or two metaphors in education not analyzed in this book.

Write a short essay on the topic suggested below:
From your school experiences select and describe an example of a classroom encounter, or course, or an entire program which in your view subscribed to the growth *or* molding metaphor. Show how the experience can be regarded as an illustration of *one* of those approaches to education and explain what the strengths and weaknesses in the approach are.

CHAPTER 3

An Analysis of the Concept of Education

One of the main purposes of this book is to arrive at a clear understanding of the concept of education and as a result be a better position to assess whether our schools are or are not educational institutions and to determine what can be done to improve them in their function as educational institutions. We have already seen in the previous discussion on the use of educational metaphors that it is very difficult to get a clear grip on the concept education. Though metaphors are somewhat helpful, they are perhaps more misleading than insightful. What is required is a full-scale conceptual analysis of the concept in line with our discussion in Chapter 1 of the philosopher's role in attacking the question of meaning. So in this chapter we will be taking a very close look at R.S. Peters' analysis, which represents the most rigorous and thoroughgoing analysis of the concept ever undertaken.

Several Uses of the Term 'Education'

Some of the confusion regarding the term 'education' stems from the fact that there are several uses of the term that have arisen out of or apart from the central notion of education and have developed a life of their own. So in order to be true to the way in which the term 'education' is used (i.e., not to stipulate or legislate, but to report faithfully) one must take these usages into account. At least three distinct uses of education can be isolated, and we shall refer to them as E_1, E_2, and E_3.

The Sociological Use (E_1)

The sociological use of 'education' has been so called because it is typically the one used by sociologists in describing the child-rearing practices of a people or society. Such description will often include schooling practices (E_2), but need not do so. Some societies do not have formal schools; the children are 'educated' at father's or mother's side or are nurtured and reared communally. They are 'educated' (acculturated, socialized) through processes ranging from apprenticeship modelling to formal didactic instruction. The important point to note is that this use of 'education' does not necessarily refer to formal schooling (the 'institutional use' referred to below as E_2) nor to the achievement of general enlightenment (referred to below under E_3). The emphasis is on practices of socializing the child into the extant culture. It matters not if the beliefs acquired are false or correct, if the practices and skills developed are or are not morally acceptable from a universalizable standpoint, nor if the outcome of the training and rearing process results in blind adherence to the doctrines and rituals of the cultural group. According to this use of the term 'educated', whoever is properly 'acculturated' (or socialized) is 'educated'. The two terms are roughly synonymous. It is this use of the term 'education' which is employed in such expressions as 'The education of Henry Adams' or 'Oliver Twist's street education'. Reference is made to any shaping of mind and character by any means whatsoever. Unlike E_3 (below) there is no reference to *good* character or *legitimate* means of socialization. The reference is to the description of the socializing practices or growing-up influences in the particular person's life regardless of the positive or negative nature of those influences. The E_1, (sociological) use of course can represent a considerable overlap with 'education' when that refers specifically to those influences on a person stemming from formal schools or institutions.

The Institutional Use (E_2)

The schooling or institutional use of the term 'education' straightforwardly represents reference to a person's development as a result of influences from schools or other formal 'educational' institutions. Common parlance relies on this use in such expressions as, 'How many years of education did you get?' (How many years did you go to school?) or 'I quit my job to continue my education' (I quit my job to return to school or university.) or 'All that education didn't do me much good' (Those years in school didn't do me much good.). It is very common in ordinary speech to refer to whatever goes on in schools as education. However — and this is important to note — at the same time, with equally legitimate use and no doubt more significant meaning, the same people will use 'education' in a more profound and thoughtful sense when they say things like 'I went to school all those years, but failed to get an education', or 'I gained a good education though I never went to school'. Here, reference is to a sense of 'education' which is neither E_1 or E_2; it is what we shall here call the 'general enlightenment' sense of education.

The 'General Enlightenment' Use (E_3)

When reference is made to 'education' as something that may or may not go on in schools (as in those uses just noted above) or may or may not result from socialization (E_1), what is being referred to is a particular kind of human achievement which is considered to be a most valuable development of mind characterized by knowledge and understanding. Such a nascent concept of education was already extant in early Greece and was referred to as *paedia*. It is the use that clearly allows one to argue that schools are or are not (should be or should not be) educational institutions. Such talk does not even make sense if 'schooling' and 'education' are considered to be synonymous; if, that is, E_2 and E_3 are collapsed. It is the use that permits one to say with sense that certain forms of socialization are (or are not) contributory to education. It is the use that clearly is central to any discussion of education which is not superficial, even if it is granted that peripheral uses of 'education', as in E_1 and E_2, are also legitimate, meaningful uses. It is the use that will concern us in the Peters analysis to follow and in the remainder of the book, particularly in the discussion of the justification of education in Chapter 10. What, then, more precisely is education in this general enlightenment sense? For a discussion of this we turn to the analysis of 'education' by R.S. Peters.

R.S. Peters' Analysis of 'Education'

Preliminary Observations

We do well to remind ourselves what the task before us is. In conceptual analysis the attempt is to elucidate a concept by making explicit the rules according to which the term functions in ordinary language. Some people find it helpful to think of this task in terms of Ryle's metaphor of mapping the logical geography of a concept. We have done some of this mapping in the previous section. Because the concept 'education' is so complex it will be impossible to provide a complete and detailed map. We shall, in the short space and time available, have to be satisfied with the main contours of the map. Stepping now out of the metaphor, we shall have to be satisfied if we are able to provide *some key* rules for the concept of education, which may be insufficient to provide a complete definition of it. The rules we do isolate, however, will be necessary and they will reflect accurately public usage. Accordingly Peters isolates three central criteria for the use of the term 'education'. Before we turn to those, it is helpful to mention a few incidental observations connected with the concept 'education'.

One such observation is that a conceptual analysis of 'education' other than Peters' is very hard to come upon. He himself has noted that 'when I was working on my Inaugural Lecture on *Education as Initiation*, (I) was unable to unearth any previous explicit attempt to demarcate the concept of "education"'.[1] It is not surprising, then, that Peters has held central stage in philosophy of education since that time. There have, of course, been numerous healthy debates concerning the completeness and accuracy of the analysis but no serious successful challenges to the central claims Peters makes regarding the value and knowledge criteria for 'education' as discussed below. But first one or two more incidental observations about education which Peters himself makes.

'Education' according to Peters is primarily an 'achievement' term. The reference here is to G. Ryle's distinction between 'achievement' (success, or 'got it') verbs, which refer to the outcome of an activity, and 'task' verbs, which specify activities.[2] Thus 'win', 'find', 'hear', 'arrive', and 'cure' are achievements corresponding respectively to the tasks of 'run', 'seek', 'listen', 'travel', and 'treat'. Achievement terms do not specify an activity; there is nothing you do when you find or arrive in addition to seeking or travelling, and so on. In like manner 'education' picks out no activities or processes (or nearly none, see below) like instructing, teaching, going to school, studying, and so on; but rather refers to the state of being for which those processes were outcomes. Strictly speaking it is wrong to say things like, 'I am educating him', for there is nothing specifiable that one necessarily does in bringing about education. Teaching is a specifiable activity, but education is not. Education is what results from having engaged in a series of activities which result in a person becoming educated. In *Ethics and Education*, Peters says that 'It (education) lays down criteria to which activities or processes must conform'.[3] A corollary of this observation is that we do not look for clarification of the concept education to the practices of so-called educational institutions but rather to the characteristics of an educated person. So, as already noted, 'education' is *primarily* an achievement term. Nevertheless, it is not entirely so. There are, as we shall see below, certain restrictions as to what counts as an educational activity, regardless of the worthwhileness of the outcome. Certain kinds of treatments of individuals are morally objectionable no matter how worthy the goal appears to be.

Two other incidental observations about education that Peters makes concern the notions of 'deliberateness' and 'initiation'. Peters talks of education as being a *deliberate* attempt on the part of someone (often a teacher) to *initiate* someone else (the student) into a hitherto unknown world of knowledge and understanding and practice (say, the world of pictorial art, or perhaps geometry). In recent years these two notions have given rise to discussion and controversy. The issue concerning deliberateness is whether or not certain worthwhile achievements in knowledge and understanding that come about non-deliberately, naturally, without effort, that are acquired almost by osmosis by living with those 'in the know', that are the result of 'picking things up', count as educational achievements. Does, for example, a person's education really begin in the crib when first distinctions are made and first words learned? Does it continue when one learns naturally to speak truthfully and to regard others? And if so, does that mean that everyone who has the qualities of personhood is therefore partially educated? Or does 'education' refer only to those school-like deliberate acts of initiation usually beginning at about age 4 to 6? And is the term *initiation* crucial in this process? Does 'initiation' refer to a particular methodology, that is, a non-rational method of teaching and holding of beliefs? And, does Peters' use of the phrase 'education as initiation' suggest such a methodology? Or is the term 'initiation' a relatively neutral term with respect to methodology? And could the term 'initiation' without shift in Peters' analysis have been replaced with a term such as 'introduction to' or 'familiarization with' or 'understanding and acceptance of', and so on? Some, for example, have argued that Peters makes room for the process of indoctrination in education because of his use of the word 'initiation'. Others have argued that Peters' use of that term is an error precisely because it leads one to such conclusions. The position taken here is that the term 'initiation' is relatively neutral and is of little consequence in Peters' scheme of things. For Peters the central features of education are the criterial attributes of (1) value and (2) knowledge. In addition there is (3) a procedural requirement. These three criteria for education are at the core of his analysis. Once the full force of these three criteria is grasped, it becomes apparent that it is of minor consequence whether the process is deliberate or not or whether the process is or is not characterized as initiation. To that core analysis we now turn.

The Value (Desirability) Criterion

Education, in the more differentiated sense of E_3 explored above, is not value-neutral according to Peters. Acquiring eduation is acquiring something worthwhile and desirable. In *Ethics and Education*, Peters writes: 'It would be a logical contradiction to say that a man had been educated but that he had in no way changed for the better'.[4] In this regard, education is like the concept 'reform'. To say that a person is reformed is to say that he has become better, *by definition*. This is a logical feature of the concept. By itself this feature does not determine which particulars are the things of value anymore than the concept 'reform' tells us which particulars make people morally better. It is a separate and uniquely difficult task to argue and support claimed about which things are valuable in education. All that is being claimed so far is that one cannot in education aovid making value judgments. Some educationists maintain that by appealing to children's needs or interests or society's needs or by recognizing developmental patterns in children or growth tendencies one can escape the awesome task of making judgments about what is educationally good or worthwhile or valuable. The escape, as we shall see again and again, is impossible. One does willy-nilly make value choices in education. One can of course be trained to do undesirable things such as lock-picking and smuggling. But to be 'educated in smuggling' is logically impossible unless one deems the skill of smuggling desirable *and* it is desirable, which would then have to be shown. Nor can one logically claim that 'all that *education* didn't do me much good', at least not in the E_3 sense of education. It is of course possible to say sensibly that 'all that *schooling* didn't do me much good' and the reasons probably would be because it didn't provide me with an education. But that would only underline the fact that education is the achievement of something of value.

Moreover, the something of value that is achieved in education is *intrinsically* valuable. Education is not merely a tool or instrument to do things with, such as to succeed in getting a job or provide one with a skill to obtain extrinsic ends. Education is valuable in itself and for its own sake. The knowledge and understanding obtained become features of one's person and shape one's sense of what is of ultimate value. Education, while it does also contribute to the means of achieving certain ends, is primarily concerned with the provision of worthwhile ends or goals of life. It is in that sense non-instrumental. Thus education is very much concerned with the ethical questions associated with the good life, as we shall see further in Chapter 10 on the question of the justification of education.

But a caution is in order. Some people, agreeing that education is through and through a values enterprise, have drawn the false conclusion that if education implies value, then value implies education. But, of course, A implies B does not imply that B implies A. Not everything of value is educational. Eating, relaxing, and playing games may all be valuable, even intrinsically valuable, but they are not educational. Educational value is to be found only within a limited, specifiable range of valuable achievements; and that range is limited by the second criterion discussed below. A great deal of nonsense is asserted about education when the several criteria of education are not taken together, when, that is, a single necessary criterion is taken in isolation and considered to be sufficient. Thus teachers or 'educational leaders' sometimes argue that certain socially valuable activities (e.g., skiing, swimming, dancing, socializing, playing games, etc.) are educational and so should be pursued in public educational institutions because they are valuable for the young people to have, forgetting that any activity that is educational *must also* fulfill the procedural requirements of the third criterion (discussed below) *but* particularly also the cognitive requirements of the knowledge criterion.

The Knowledge Criterion

The fact that educated people are knowledgeable is not merely an interesting observation about some people; it is a definitional truth. If someone attempted to display to you an educated person who knew next to nothing, you would not marvel at the curious finding but charge him with failure to make sense, with failure to understand language. Education without knowledge is logically impossible. That much seems undisputable and straightforward. But the questions of how much and what kinds of knowledge are required for education engender considerable dispute and raise complex issues. Peters' claim is that education requires knowledge in breadth and depth in a manner commanding our commitment and concern. We shall look at these claims in turn, for the knowledge criterion is clearly central in any analysis of education and the key to understanding Peters' analysis.

Breadth

How much must a person know to be considered educated? There can only be a vague answer to this question, for there exist no clear criteria for determining this. It is better to think of education as an ideal which no one can fully achieve, since no one can know everything. On the other end of the continuum it is clear that very few normal people know nothing. So almost everyone is partially educated since we all have some knowledge. Nevertheless we do talk about educated and uneducated people and mean something by this. So if one insists on pressing the point and demanding an answer, the best that can be done is point to a relatively arbitrary norm for a particular society representing an average achievement in knowledge below which people would be considered uneducated and above which, educated. But that question is relatively unimportant in the breadth issue. What is crucial is the spread in types of knowledge. An educated person is one who has mastered a wide range of types of knowledge. The more narrow the focus in knowledge the more we are inclined to withhold the appellation 'educated'. A scientist who knew everything about quasars but nothing about aesthetics, history, or ethics — were that possible — would not win a citation for being educated, no matter how well-trained he was. The minimum breadth requirement is comprehension of and familiarization with *all* the logical types of knowledge — those 'forms of knowledge and understanding' discussed in Chapter 5, namely, logic, empirical science, human science, aesthetics, ethics, and philosophy (and perhaps religion). An education omitting any one of these 'forms' is deficient. Narrowness and education are antithetical. The point can be made even more strikingly by contrasting education with training.

One of the key ideas in understanding the notion 'training' is narrowness of focus. This narrowness is related both to the simple nature of the achievement and to the paucity of rational understanding and cognitive implications required for mastery. Usually training refers to those activities in education which are instrumental in the achievement of major educational goals. We are trained *in* reading and times tables, in sharpening pencils and tying shoelaces, in handling scientific experimental equipment and in pole vaulting. But we become educated persons by mastering understanding of science and literature, of aesthetic form and body functions. The commonplace distinction between physical *training* and physical *education* illustrates the above-noted contrasting features. Even more dramatic is the distinction between sex education and sex training. Very few devotees of sex education, which suggests wide understanding of the complex problems surrounding that subject, are advocates of sex training, which suggests narrowly defined skills with minimum cognition.

The breadth requirement for education also answers to the frequent demand for *wholeness* in education. Educating the whole child is a conceptual truth about education; it is not an option which only some schools, for example, the Waldorf schools, subscribe to. And the wholeness relates not only to breadth of knowledge and cognitive content but also to feeling and emotion. As we shall see further below (in 'Intellectualism'), educational achievement is not merely cold intellectual understanding but an acquisition of corresponding appropriate emotions and attitudes. Such change in emotions and attitude come about because the depth requirement for knowledge has also been satisfied.

Depth

The educated person has more than superficial acquaintance with many free-floating bits of knowledge. Peters often speaks of knowledge together with understanding as a single requirement for education. There is a reason for this. As an analysis of knowledge shows (see 'The Nature of Knowledge' in Chapter 5), knowledge is justified, true belief; and without grasping (or understanding) the justification for belief there can be no genuine knowledge. It is this understanding that gives depth to the whole enterprise of knowledge acquisition in education. This is why Peters writes of the educated person as one who sees the 'reason why' of things and approaches knowledge from the 'inside of a way of thought'; he has grasped the principles for organizing facts and the conceptual schemes which give coherence to otherwise disjointed 'inert' knowledge. Depth and breadth ultimately complement each other and give one 'cognitive perspective', and ability to see connections between various forms of knowledge and how they play a part in a unified and coherent way of life. Thus for the educated person knowledge has direct impact on one's attitude and direction in life. It transforms one's outlook and adds dimensions to one's person. And since knowledge plays such an important role in life one becomes committed to the pursuit of truth, caring about detail and evidence with a keenness not characteristic of the uneducated. Such concern for evidence is also characteristic of the manner in which education is brought about.

The Procedural Criterion

As noted in the section on 'Preliminary observations', education is primarily an achievement term. The value and knowledge criteria discussed above represent that achievement. There is, however, a task aspect to education as well. This task aspect relates to the appropriateness of the procedures for bringing about education. According to Peters the procedures (various kinds of activities such as teaching, instructing, or attending school) must be consistent with the ends to be achieved. Such activities, or processes, are legion; one cannot name them all. Almost anything will count as an educational procedure as long as two conditions are met: (1) the procedure must result in an educationally valuable achievement, and (2) the manner of proceeding must not infringe upon the wittingness and voluntariness on the part of the learner or achiever. This second condition does not rule out compulsion, commanding, coercion and the like (if for good reasons they are justified), for the learner in these instances still has a choice and can resist instruction. However, if methods such as conditioning, indoctrinating, and brain washing and the like are employed, then the learner cannot resist. These are ruled out on moral grounds, according to Peters, and do not count as educational procedures. So this third criterion is a negative one; it does not tell us in any specific ways what is required as a procedure for education but tells us only what is not permitted.

If we now put the three criteria for education together we can construct a rough definition for education as follows: education is the achievement of a desirable state of mind characterized by knowledge and understanding in breadth and depth with cognitive perspective and by corresponding appropriate emotions and attitudes, these brought about, deliberately, in a manner not to infringe upon the voluntariness and wittingness on the part of the learner. The above, allowing for error and misconstrual of interpretation, is the analysis that Peters gives. It has withstood severe and multifold criticism and can, with only minor adjustment, be considered acceptable. Some of the criticism that has been levied can be usefully discussed to gain further insight into the concept.

Critical Remarks on Peters' Analysis

Necessity of the Three Conditions

In *The Logic of Education*, Peters himself, with Hirst, considers whether the desirability condition for education can be dropped.[5] He considers counter-examples in which people use the term 'education' as though it is a bad state to be in. These people consider it bad because they equate 'education' with books and theories and what goes on in schools and universities. They have the E_2 sense of education discussed above. And because what the books and theories provide is thought of as either a waste of time or undermining favourite doctrines and practices of their particular cultural tradition, 'education' is thought of as bad. There is then a use of 'education' in which the desirability condition is absent. But of course, as Peters and Hirst show, and as also argued here, that is not a genuine counter example, for the desirability condition applies only to the E_3 sense, the differentiated and more precise sense of education. In that differentiated sense the desirability condition is a necessary one. And this can be maintained even if it is granted that in the E_2 schooling sense it is correct to remark that the education (i.e., schooling) was a bad experience.

One objection not dealt with there, nor apparently anywhere, is the possible redundancy of the third, procedural condition. It will be recalled that the third condition is the one that rules out as education any procedures such as conditioning and indoctrination on the grounds that they infringe upon the voluntariness on the part of the learner and are thus ruled out on *moral* grounds. It will here be argued that such a move is redundant since such procedures are already ruled out on *logical* grounds required by the knowledge condition. It is doubtful that conditioning is always immoral. Acquiring toilet habits through a process of conditioning in early childhood surely is an acceptable and desirable practice. It is not immoral. But then it is also not considered education in the E_3 sense because of the absence of understanding and reasoned justification, as required by the knowledge condition. Now if education requires knowledge, not merely skill; and if knowledge is having beliefs which are true and which are justified by good reasons and evidence and recognized so to be justified; then it could never be the case that such beliefs could ever be acquired through a process of conditioning or brain washing or indoctrination, for these procedures never can in principle permit such cognition and understanding. If such understanding of the evidence does occur it is a sure sign that conditioning, and so on, did not. So the nefarious procedures are already ruled out by the strict requirements of the knowledge condition; and so the third criterion is strictly speaking redundant. It may, however, *also* be the case that certain forms of conditioning and other procedures such as indoctrination are immoral for other reasons. For these other reasons and for convenience we shall continue to make reference to the third, procedural condition, even if only for sake of emphasis.

Intellectualism

Another form of criticism brought against Peters is that his analysis fails to take into account those elements of education concerning emotional development. The analysis, it is thought, is too intellectual, emphasizing as it does the cognitive components of education at the expense of development of the whole child. This charge, however, really rests on failure fully to understand Peters' position. As already alluded to in the section on 'Breadth', there is ample scope and demand for emotional development occurring concurrently with cognitive development. It is in fact part of Peters' broader educational theory that the two cannot be separated. In *Ethics and Education* Peters argues that emotions are not self-subsistent entities cut adrift from cognitions.[6] Emotions have a cognitive core; and depending on how we appraise certain situations (e.g., snakes are dangerous) we do or do not feel fear or anxiety. There is, in other words, always a cognitive aspect to emotions and an emotive aspect to cognitions. We do not, for example, study the cognitive elements of a poem on one day and the emotional elements of it on the next. To have understood the poem is at the same time to have been able to respond to it emotionally in the appropriate way. So when education emphasizes cognition it is not omitting the emotive and feeling side of human beings. Development of feeling and attitude is part and parcel of development of knowledge and understanding.

Elitism

Closely related to the above criticism of 'intellectualism' is the alleged 'elitism' in a form of education that emphasizes knowledge in breadth and depth, particularly theoretical knowledge as required by the justification condition of knowledge. Apparently some people hold and argue that an education that emphasizes knowledge in breadth and depth favors certain children (the brighter ones) and certain segments of society (the professions), in which many bright people work. It is thought that there is a basic injustice in a system which allows some children to perform better than others. To correct the injustice it is advocated that certain children should be permitted to spend a fair portion of their time in school (and the slowest, almost all of their time) in pursuit for practical skills for employment and leisure, while the brighter youngsters only are left to pursue primarily 'academic' knowledge. In this way everyone has an opportunity to 'succeed' in school and thus the basic injustice is remedied.

Now if this argument is difficult to understand it is because it doesn't make much sense. If there is an injustice here, it is certainly not of man's making; rather it might be considered some sort of cosmic injustice about which we can do very little. It just is the case that some children perform better than others in any given area of human endeavour. The random distribution of talent at birth is a given and it is impossible to engineer equal achievement. Achieving equal amounts of different things does not represent removal of injustice any more than does achieving different amounts of the same thing. To say *a* achieves the same amount of *x* as *b* achieves of *y* is not to say that *a* and *b* have something of equal value. If it is *education* that is of such supreme value, it cannot be replaced with something else, *training*, for example, and the outcome deemed of equal value and equal achievement. Just because some people because of innate capabilities achieve more education than others with lesser capability, it does not follow that the latter should be cheated of what is after all of the highest value. Are those who would argue otherwise prepared to condemn large segments of our population to ignorance and cultural deprivation? If so, that would indeed be an unjustifiable inequality of educational opportunity. Inequality is not inherent in a concept of education which emphasizes knowledge and understanding as intrinsically valuable for everybody.

Because education is so valuable for everybody, education should be the central concern of the school. That does not mean that schools could not also be concerned with other matters. What the school's role in society is, however, must not be confused with what the role of education is in a person's life and in the community. To these issues, often referred to as the aims of education, we turn next.

Recommended further readings:

HIRST, P.H. and PETERS, R.S. (1970) *op. cit.*, pp. 17–25.
PETERS, R.S. (1966) 'Criteria of education' in *Ethics and Education*, George Allen and Unwin, pp. 23–45.
BARROW, R. and WOODS, R. (1982) 'The concept of education' in *An Introduction to Philosophy of Education* (2nd Edition), London, Methuen, pp. 9–22.

Notes

1 PETERS, R.S. (1967) 'What is an educational process?' in *The Concept of Education*, London, Routledge and Kegan Paul, p. 1.
2 See RYLE, G. (1966) *The Concept of Mind*, London, Hutchison, pp. 149–53.
3 PETERS, R.S. (1966) *Ethics and Education*, London, George Allen and Unwin, p. 25.
4 PETERS, R.S., *ibid.*, p. 25.
5 HIRST, P.H. and PETERS, R.S. (1970) *op. cit.*, pp. 17–25.
6 PETERS, R.S. (1966) *op. cit.*, pp. 110ff.

Questions and Exercises

R.S. Peters states that education 'picks out no particular activity or process. Rather it lays down criteria to which activities or processes must conform' (*Ethics and Education*, p. 25). Briefly summarize the three criteria made explicit by Peters. How adequate are they for the notion of 'general liberal education'? Are there uses of 'education' to which these criteria do not apply?

Provide brief answers to the following questions:

1 What does it mean to say that education is an 'achievement term'?
2 How would you differentiate between 'training' and 'education'? Is it possible to train and educate simultaneously? Explain, giving examples.
3 In what ways is the concept 'education' like the concept 'reform'?
4 Are there senses in which 'education' is a neutral term?
5 Are there any limits as to what counts as an educational task?
6 Learning to ski may be valuable, even intrinsically valuable. Is it therefore necessarily educational? Could it be educational? Explain.
7 Is Peters' 'procedural' criterion for education redundant? Explain.

What would be wrong with saying the following:

1 'He should know better, for I was educating him all day.'
2 'She is educated, but it hasn't done her much good.'
3 'I hope to get my education while under hypnosis.'
4 'During my education I was conditioned to believe that the army had better food than the civilians during the Great War.'

CHAPTER 4

'Aims' in Education

In this chapter we do not wish merely to talk about the 'aims of education', if there are such things, but about how the term 'aims' is used in educational discourse as well as about the role and function of schools, and how schooling and education are distinguished.

The Logic of 'Aim'

First let us consider some general features of the concept 'aim'.[1] The term 'aim' is typically used to refer to actions or activities of thinking beings who have intentions. Thus guns *point*, but people *aim*. Further the term is applied to actions which are instrumental in bringing something else about. All human action is either (a) instrumental to the achievement of something else or (b) worthwhile in itself. 'Aims' always refer to instrumental actions. We ask for the aim of an activity when we want to know what state of affairs that activity is to bring about or what ends it serves. When an activity is done for its own sake, it is very odd to ask for its aim. We do not ask what the aim is of my enjoying myself playing tennis. Another point about the logic of 'aims' is that we ask for aims in contexts where we think it is important to get people to specify more precisely what they are trying to do. 'Aims' suggest concentration of attention and effort toward an object not too close at hand and easily obtained, that is, in situations where failure is possible. They differ from ideals in that respect. So it makes good sense to ask, What is the aim of the school? but not, What is the aim of cooking? In the latter case, the question is absurd because the point of cooking is obvious and requires no focused concentration. But what about the aim(s) of education? It is not entirely clear that it makes sense to talk this way about education in the E_3 sense. On the one hand it seems that sharpening of focus is very much required. On the other hand it is not necessary that education have a purpose beyond itself. Also, because education is not an activity at all, but rather an achievement, it is doubtful that it makes sense to talk of the aim of education. To put it succinctly, since talk of 'aims' is limited to activities, but education is not an activity; then it is a logical mistake to talk of the aims of education. Mistake or not, the worry or uneasiness about the point of pursuing education won't go away. Why is that? Perhaps it is because we have heretofore dealt insufficiently with the full force and meaning of knowledge in depth and breadth, as required for education in the E_3 sense. If it could be shown that knowledge is central in the development of mind, and that development of mind is crucial in one's development as a person, then much of the puzzle over the point of education disappears, for one does not puzzle over the point and purpose of developing as a person.

Development of Persons as the Aim of Education

A number of philosophers of education have argued that education is tantamount to the development of persons. Foremost among these is Paul Hirst, who argues roughly as follows: (a) education is the achievement of various forms of knowledge; (b) achievement of knowledge is necessary for the development of rationality; (c) the achievement of rationality is tantamount to those achievements characteristic of persons; so (d) education, because it is tantamount to the achievement of rationality, is tantamount to the development of persons.[2] Because rationality is self-justifying no further justification for education is necessary. The aim of education is thus transparent.

That, in skeletal form, is the argument we want to elaborate upon and discuss and criticize in this section. Our previous discusion of education revealed that one key criterion for education is knowledge and understanding in breadth. This breadth requires some degree of mastery of *all* the logical types of knowledge. By the phrase 'form of knowledge and experience' Hirst and Peters mean all those extant ways in which we make rational sense of the world and our experience in it. These 'forms' do not collapse into or correspond on a one-to-one basis to standard disciplines or school subjects. Disciplines and subjects are administrative arrangements centered around interesting problems and topics; but ultimately they are made up of these forms. The forms rather represent discrete conceptual schemes and distinct canons of verifiability. According to Hirst there are seven such forms: (1) logic and pure mathematics, (2) empirical (physical) science, (3) social (human) science and history, (4) aesthetics, (5) morality and ethics, (6) philosophy, and (7) possibly religion, although there is a problem with verifiability in religion. These seven forms, then, represent all the possible ways in which we can make rational sense of the world. When we know a particular proposition we know it because we have understood certain clusters of concepts and accepted certain ways of supporting or grounding claims with appropriate evidence. There are then these different ways of being rational and being aware. So knowledge is not just a tool we have to employ in our thinking and to furnish our minds with. What we know are the constituents of our minds. To a large extent we are what we know. Central to the notion of mind is the concept of consciousness or awareness. What differentiates things with minds (such as people) from things without minds (such as machines) is the fact that the former are aware (conscious) and the latter not. The peculiar thing about consciousness is that to be conscious one has to be conscious of something. One cannot be conscious of, or about, nothing. But things about which one can be conscious have to have an identity, a limitation, a restriction, or circumference which picks them out from the ooze of pre-conscious mush and identifies them as recognizable entities. What is it that enables us to select these objects of consciousness? Concepts; and propositions made up of concepts. The very possibility of our experiencing anything in the world is our conceptualization of something. Peters writes:

> The ideas and expectations of an individual centre of consciousness . . . do not develop as deposits out of an ato-mic individual experience. . . . On the contrary they are the product of the initiation of an individual into public tradi-tions enshrined in the language, concepts, beliefs and rules of a society.[3]

This view of the origin and development of mind is very different from the British empirical tradition, as represented by the *tabula rasa* notion of Locke, and from the American emphasis on experi-ence, as represented by Dewey's reliance on experience as the key to educational success. The problem with Locke's 'blank slate' is that the principle for selecting the sense data that makes recognition of an entity possible is missing. The problem with relying on experience as the method for recognizing entities and learning new ideas is that experience presupposes the concepts which are thus to be learnt. Kant was most lucid and logical in suggesting that concepts and categories imposed a kind of order on the flux of sense data to enable intelligent experience and awareness to occur. Without concepts meaningful experience is impossible. A tiny baby touring New York on the back of a parent has not, despite open eyes, experienced New York. It simply does not have the conceptual apparatus. The problem with Kant, however, is that he (and others — Chomsky, for example) believed we were born with the conceptual apparatus already nascent in us as a 'deep structure'. A more reasonable assumption, one that Peters articulates in *Ethics and Education*, is that the conceptual rules and structures are learnt (perhaps) or acquired (certainly) in the process of associating with our parents and elders. They are precipitates of the social experience of being initiated into public language and symbol systems. It is not the case that we first learn concepts and later have experience, nor that we first have experience and from that learn concepts. Rather they occur together. Again, Peters is worth quoting on this important issue:

> The objects of consciousness are first and foremost objects in a public world that are marked out and differentiated by a public language into which the individual is initiated. The learning of language and the discovery of a public world of objects in space and time proceed together.... The individual's consciousness, as well as his individuality, is neither intelligible nor genetically explicable without the public world which he is conscious of, in relation to which he develops, and on which he imprints his own individual style and pattern of being.[4]

The name of the process whereby an individual is guided into various forms of conceptual structures, various forms of knowledge and awareness (and all this is equivalent to developing a mind) is education, for which the term initiation applies so appositely. A brief description of how Peters sees this development occurring in the history of an individual person is as follows:

1 Early on as a baby the child has no recognizable conscious states. At best a new-born infant has inchoate wishes.
2 A little later the child develops awareness (perhaps, first, of

mother), but this is not yet differentiated into beliefs, wants, and specific emotions.

3 As the child matures he acquires a richer mode of awareness through the acquisition of plans, rules, reasons associated with goals, information, causal connections, and an understanding of means-ends relationships, and so on.

4 A more fully developed person has acquired knowledge of various sorts, has a perspective on the many things he has learnt, has regard for and cares about truth standards, and has understanding of underlying reasons and causes.

In other words the person has become educated, and in doing so has developed fully as a person. The process of education has opened up to him a vast inheritance of knowledge and understanding accumulated by those versed in the more specific modes of thought and awareness such as science, logic, history, aesthetics, morals, and philosophy.

Now the reason the above depiction of the development of mind, if true (and it should not be thought that the last word has been said about this controversial issue), can be thought of as simultaneously developing the person is that a person is someone who *is* (not *has*) a unity of mind and body. A person without a mind is a person in name only and is so called, perhaps, only for social and moral reasons. Now if it is correct so to think of a person, then the development of mind is one aspect of the development of persons. Education then becomes the key to understanding how a person develops. Who I am is largely the result of what sort of an education I got. If a certain 'form of knowledge and awareness' is omitted in my education, then I am to that extent deficient as a person. It can be said of Hitler and others like him that they are inhuman to the extent that the form of ethical understanding was omitted in their education. Other people are thought bizarre and underdeveloped because they lack aesthetic understanding; some are thought to be 'crazy' because they have no sense of the 'real' world around them, and so on. A fully developed person has a full complement of all the available forms of knowledge and awareness; he has a well-rounded education.

The view that education is tantamount to the development of persons rests on a number of assumptions. The first is that mind is not inborn. This is an empirical thesis based on observation of infants. The second is that mind is an essential attribute of being a person. This is a logical thesis. It claims that mental capacities such as reasoning ability, self-consciousness, emotional capacities, capa-

city to desire and change desires, capability of speech and conceptualization and so on, are the most important features of persons. A
third assumption is that mind is best developed in the early years
through a process of inculcation approximating apprenticeship learning, and in the more mature phases of development through a
process of deliberate initiation, primarily by teaching. This is also
an empirical assumption. Finally the theory assumes that learning
from experience presupposes conceptual categories to make experience possible. This also is a logical thesis. Since these are reasonable
assumptions to make, the view that education is the development of
persons also seems reasonable.

There is, however, also a reasonable objection to holding such a
view. The objection can be stated roughly as follows: in order to be
in a position to acquire knowledge one must already be rational in
the minimal sense of having the dispositions to be consistent, to
assess statements on relevant considerations, and to be critical of
one's beliefs. These minimal conditions of rationality are sufficient
for characterizing anyone as a person. And since education is the
acquisition of worthwhile knowledge, it must be the case that only
persons can receive education. Hence education is *not* the development of mind and persons, since these are presupposed for education to take place.[6]

Such an objection is well taken; but does not really defeat the
main thesis above. The objection addresses the problem of the
genesis of rationality and personhood, whereas what has been described in this section is about *development* of rationality and personhood. Since the term 'development' is used to refer to both these
phenomena it is easy to let that ambiguity mislead us. The question
of how rationality begins, and how knowledge and rationality can
get off the ground when they seem to presuppose each other — these
questions about the inception of rationality — are quite different
from the issue of how rationality grows and develops once it has
begun, the latter being the process of education as described by
Hirst and Peters. This distinction between the genesis and the development of rationality is parallel to the distinction between *becoming a person* and *developing as a person*. In the one sense of
development, then, it is wrong to say that education is the development of persons, where that means the process of becoming a
person. But in the other sense of development it is correct to make
the claim, where it means developing as a person. Becoming a
person is similar to the gradual acquisition of those rational capacities essential for personhood-consciousness, intentionality, purpo-
siveness, speech, argument, and so on. These develop in an infant in

some minimal sense very early on in life through some unexplained process (perhaps of initiation and modelling) not typical of deliberate teaching and learning in an educational engagement. If this is correct then the identification of education with *becoming a person* is too strong. Education is not an engagement in which non-persons are turned into persons. It is after all persons whom we educate. Nevertheless, it is still correct to say that education is helping people to become more fully persons by acquiring in a more complete way those powers of rationality which a young child possesses only in a minimal and undeveloped way. In this sense education can still correctly be thought of as development of persons. In acquiring an education one is becoming a different person while still remaining the same person. And it is this in Hirst's and Peters' arguments that is worth emphasizing with respect to aims in education.

Once it is understood that education is the development of mind, of rationality, and of persons it is also easily understood why the value of education is intrinsic to education and why it is otiose to ask for the aims of education. For is there a conceivable end beyond the development as a person for which that development could be a means?

Yet people continue to ask with apparent meaning and seriousness of concern for the aims of education. From the school principal's office to the education editor's desk of the local newspaper we are constantly being admonished to examine and review and establish aims of education. What, then, is the meaning behind these concerns? For an answer we turn to an examination of how the phrase 'aims of education' can be interpreted.

Interpreting 'Aims of Education'

Various possible interpretations can be given the question, 'What are the aims of education?' It depends very much on circumstance, context, and questioner as to what is being referred to in any particular instance. There is, first, a meaning of the question which is similar to 'What is the meaning of "education"?' The request is for clarification of the concept 'education'. This has its parallel to questions about the aim of reform. If in response to that, one were to say that the aim of reform is to make people better one would be expressing a definition of 'reform'. In effect the statement 'The aim of reform is to make men better' is a tautology masquerading as an aim. And in a similar way the request for the aim of education is a request for the meaning of education. Answers to such requests are not very informative if one already knows the meaning. They might nevertheless serve as reminders about what the task of education is.

A second interpretation of the question concerns the multiplicity of criterial attributes of education, and is a request for direction about what is to be emphasized in education at a particular time. Depending on an imbalance created at different periods in history, different aims will emerge as the focus for attention to correct the imbalance. Such imbalance may be regarding the task or achievement aspect of education, as when Dewey emphasized the importance of child-centeredness in education in juxtaposition to mastery of content. This would be a clear case of drawing attention to the importance of Peters' third (procedural) criterion. For Dewey the need to observe and respect the child as a person became paramount. So for him the 'aim of education' was growth and development. At other times the imbalance may concern the lop-sidedness of content, as when science and mathematics become the main focus of student achievement. The imbalance is to be corrected by focusing on the arts and literature. Thus the 'aim of education' becomes 'development of the whole child'. Dewey's remarks on aims in this context is most helpful:

> For the statement of aim is a matter of emphasis at a given time. And we do not emphasize things that do not require emphasis — we tend rather to frame our statement on the basis of defects and needs of a contemporary situation; we take for granted, without explicit statement, which would be no use, whatever is right or approximately so.[7]

So the request for aims on this interpretation is a request for a clear statement about what is to be emphasized in education at this time.

A third interpretation for 'What is the aim of education?' is 'What is the purpose of a specific activity *in* education?' The former question is simply mistaken for the latter. Whereas the logic of 'aims *of* education' is questionable, the phrase 'aims *in* education' is most sensible and to be encouraged. Here the meaning clearly concerns teaching and learning goals or objectives when reference is to a smaller subset of the wider concern of education. We might often ask, with absolute clarity and serious concern, such questions as: What is the aim of doing this experiment? . . . of individualizing instruction? . . . of going on a field trip? and so on. The request is for articulation of the appropriateness of a specific teaching act or activity in the school context within the understood wider purpose of bringing about education.

Fourthly, the request for aims of education could be viewed as a request for the justification of education. Some people are fully aware of the meaning of education but are nevertheless puzzled about which particular knowledge is worthwhile and in particular the reasons why certain forms of knowledge are important. They want to know why science is more important than technology, why poetry rather than comic books, why nutrition rather than cooking. The request is for justification, for reasons and strong argument that support such claims. This is a most understandable and laudable concern, but it is perhaps mistakenly referred to as a concern about the 'aims of education'. Chapter 10 is concerned with the question of justification.

Still another interpretation, the fifth, of the question 'What is the aim of education?' is 'What are the instrumental uses of education?' It is in response to such an interpretation that one is inclined to say, 'Education has no aims'; for the assumption in the question thus interpreted is that unless one can point to a beneficial effect of having been educated, then education is not worth pursuing. Education then is 'useless'. This emphasis on utility denies the worthwhileness of education for its own sake. Now it probably is true that certain effects of being educated have utility and serve other ends. It would be surprising if an educated person could do nothing better or could not perform certain skills that might be employable and thus help to earn money for living. But that would not make the *raison d'être* of education employability, as many people erroneously think. The error is that the question of 'What is the use of it?' is legitimate to ask about education. It is to think of education as a merchandizable product, as an investment in the monetary sense, as an instrument for other uses. From the perspective of the individual the personal gain stemming from education is viewed in terms of job success, prestige, escape from physical labour, high pay, and so on. From the perspective of the community the pay-off in education is thought to be good citizenship, social cohesiveness, and (depending on one's social philosophy) perhaps social levelling, democratic practice, equality, change, or mental health and adjustment. From the perspective of business, education is thought of as an instrument of training to keep the wheels of industry moving, to keep the economy going, to select and prepare young people for occupations and professions. What is common to all these perspectives is the view that unless education has some such demonstrable pay-off it is a waste and not worthy of pursuit. To such people the notion that education is intrinsically worthwhile because it develops the mind and the person is foreign and strange.

Finally, the request for aims of education could be, and most frequently is, thought of as 'What are the aims of the school?' In this interpretation, 'education' is thought of in the E_2 (education as schooling) sense. Such request makes a great deal of sense and is a serious concern requiring thoughtful and satisfactory responses. Debates and discussion about the role of the school in society are frequent, are healthy, and are often quite heated. This is understandable since so much time, effort, and money is devoted to schooling. There is of course no reason why a school could not perform roles in addition to education; and it most certainly does. Some of these roles will be discussed in the section to follow. The key question to be addressed in discussions about the 'aims of schooling' is: What is the ideal mixture of educational and non-educational goals for the school to pursue? The position that will be argued below and in Chapter 10 (on the justification of education) and throughout the book is that the *primary* goal of the school is education. This goal is so important that if all other goals were to be abandoned it alone would be sufficient for the schools to exist and function; and, contrarily, if the goal of education were to be lost sight of there would be almost no reason for the present public system to continue. But given that we have public schools devoted to education, there is no reason why the institution could not also fulfill certain other roles besides education. It is instructive to consider what some of these other roles might be.

The Role of the School in Society

Before noting specific roles of the school it is important to be aware of certain ambiguities in the concept 'role'. It is often sociologists who discuss the 'role' of the school, since they typically intend to provide a complete description of the effects of schooling on society. They do not always distinguish between what people intend schools to achieve and what is in fact the result of having schools. The term 'role' covers both of those ideas. Even the term 'function' is ambiguous in the same way. We can speak of 'function' when we mean 'purpose', as when we say, 'The function of the school is general enlightenment'. But we also speak of 'function' when we refer to causal or logical connections, as in 'x is the function of y', or when we refer to unintended outcomes, as when we say, 'The function of equal educational opportunity is unequal educational achievement'. So it is important to distinguish between the planned, purposeful curriculum and the unplanned, unintended 'hidden curriculum'. Studies in the social sciences are particularly important ·in discovering and bringing into the open the hidden effects, the unintended consequences, the 'functions' of the school which are not its primary purposes. Thus teachers are sometimes astounded to find that the primary learning that has occurred under their tutelage is toleration of boredom and submission to authority. It is important to weigh the unintended consequences against the intended achievements to assess whether the overall result is as positive as possible. It may, for example, be impossible to avoid a certain amount of boredom and hard work in the process of gaining knowledge and understanding, and so the unintended consequences might be worth tolerating. In other cases not. But it is always important to be as aware as possible of a school's functions in its entirety.

One further distinction to be noted is the difference between primary and secondary purposes. Even when a school is aware of its unintended functions, it must also keep in priority its purposes. A school can and does have a number of compatible purposes. It *can* have as its primary purpose general enlightenment (as discussed under 'The general enlightenment use') with the secondary purpose being provision of generalizable skills (clear writing, mathematical computation, scientific experimentation) useable in employment. It *can* also reverse that, and emphasize employable skills, letting general education in a much more impoverished form be the secondary purpose. Which of the two scenarios just cited (and which of a vast number of other possibilities) a school or a school system adopts will be a fundamental plank in the school's 'philosophy of education'. It is, in a democratic society, finally up to the people through their representatives to decide this.

With the above distinctions in mind it is now possible to enumerate some of the many possible roles of the school in society under three categories: primary purposes, secondary purposes, and unintended functions. There will be no attempt to list these in any priority nor to present an exhaustive and accurate description of what they are in fact. The items are presented merely as candidates for consideration of purposes, and as partial and typical description of some functions.

Primary Purposes

Listed below are a number of purposes the school can fulfill which are considered primary by the author. Other writers will have different suggestions. That is only to be expected of such a highly controversial subject. The point of the exercise is to present candidates for consideration. The argument for selecting the first as *the* primary purpose is given in Chapter 10.

1 The pursuit of general enlightenment. This has sometimes been phrased as liberal education. It has already been stated that this aim is so overarching and important that it alone is sufficient to justify the existence of schools.

2 Moral education, which is really a subset of (1) above, but mentioned here separately for emphasis. Chapter 9 will present a full explanation of the content and procedure of moral education.

3 Maintenance of the dominant culture, where that represents, and overlaps with, the ideals of general enlightenment or at least does not conflict with it. Thus the official language of a country, the law of the land, and a democratic form of government would be considered ideals to be transmitted by the school.

4 Creation of new knowledge (primarily in universities).

Secondary Purposes

The following are candidates to be considered as purposes to be pursued in schools but only to the extent that they do not interfere radically with the primary purposes.

1 Development and allocation of manpower. (This will have unintended consequence of grading and screening people with the effect of directing them into so-called social classes, depending on the justice of the financial reward systems in a society.)

2 Socialization, the inculcation of norms of social behavior other than moral requirements. Sometimes this aim is referred to as developing social skills, or learning to cope adeptly in society, or just 'good citizenship' and sociability.

3 Physical training and development.

    4   Distribution of social goods such as health services (inoculations, sight and hearing tests), food (milk and lunches), bursaries, counselling (personal and career), and entertainment.

    5   Training for leisure-time activities.

    6   Peace and democratic ideals.

    7   Maintenance of sub-group cultures.

    8   Preparation for change and progress, where the latter refers to greater social equality and solving such social problems as ecological imbalance.

    9   Development of creative capacity.

  10   Consumer awareness.

  11   Social mobility.

  12   Creation of new knowledge (a secondary purpose in schools and colleges).

  13   Development of leadership qualities.

Unintended Functions of the School

It has already been observed that sometimes the pursuit of 'pure' education has unexpected consequences. Some of these are laudable, others most unfortunate. Even though some of them are unfortunate, they are tolerated because they are unavoidable and constitute the price to be paid for the achievement of something most worthwhile. They are the proverbial pain for the long-term gain. The following are only some of the frequently observed unintended functions of the school.

    1   Courtship and development of attitudes to opposite sex.

    2   Baby-sitting service. (This can also be a secondary purpose of schools.)

    3   Decreasing unemployment by keeping young people out of the labour market.

    4   Personal growth and development of potential.

    5   Development of attitudes to authority.

    6   Development of compliance and submissiveness.

    7   Creation of social inequality because of equal educational opportunity.

    8   Creation of social equality because of unequal educational opportunity.

Having looked briefly at the kinds of things schools might aim at doing, either as their primary or secondary purposes, and taking into account unintended functions of schools, the stage is set for arguments to be mounted for a particular combination of roles for the school in a particular society, given that the society has not gone the route of deschooling. An example of such an argument, which is not primarily philosophical but belongs in the realms of social and political policy, has been presented by Robin Barrow's *The Philosophy of Schooling*. After rejecting proposals that the school should be concerned with being 'relevant', 'useful', or 'realistic', Barrow presents his view of what being educated means and then argues that the school should be devoted to education; socialization; child-minding; broad (not specific) vocational training which does not interfere with education; primary instruction in reading, writing and numeracy; physical training; emotional education; and, as an incidental function, social role selection. The discussion is a good example (if brief) of how to go about arguing what schools should do. It does not represent the final answer, nor one that is being accepted here. But it illustrates that it makes good sense to talk about the aims of schooling. That, however, as we have already noted, is an entirely different notion from the aims of education.

Suggested further readings:

BARROW, R. (1981) 'Schooling: Its nature and point' in *The Philosophy of Schooling*, Brighton, Wheatsheaf Books Ltd., pp. 32–7; 47–8; 49–73.
HIRST, P.H. and PETERS R.S. (1970) *op. cit.*, pp. 25–32 and 106–13.
PETERS, R.S. (1972) Must an educator have an aim?' in *Authority, Responsibility and Education*, London, George Allen and Unwin, pp. 122–31.

Notes

1 Much of what is here submitted is drawn from PETERS, R.S. (1966) *Ethics and Education*, pp. 27–30, and 'Must an educator have an aim?' in *Authority, Responsibility* and *Education*, George Allen and Unwin, 1959.
2 See several of his essays in his *Knowledge and the Curriculum*, Routledge and Kegan Paul, London, 1974.
3 PETERS, R.S. (1966) *op. cit.*, p. 48.
4 *Ibid.*, Chapter 2.
5 *Ibid.*, p. 50.
6 For such an argument, see MORGAN, J. 'Paul Hirst: Education as the development of rationality', thesis (unpublished) Simon Fraser University.

7   DEWEY, J. (1916) *Democracy and Education*, New York, Macmillan, p. 130.
8   See BARROW, R. (1981) *The Philosophy of Schooling*, Brighton, Wheatsheaf Books Ltd., pp. 32–73.

Questions and Exercises

Answer the following as briefly as possible:
1   Is it a logical mistake to talk about the 'aims of education'? Explain.
2   Would you consider development of the person to be an aim of education? Explain in some detail.
3   What is the distinction between aims 'of' education and aims 'in' education? Illustrate appropriate uses for each.
4   Should schools be strictly educational institutions? Should they be educational institutions primarily?
5   Some people hold the view that education is roughly equivalent to the development of persons. What assumptions do they make? Are they warranted in their assumptions?

Write an essay of about two thousand words on the following topic/ question:
It is generally accepted that one of the school's functions is the preparation and allocation of manpower. Is this function incompatible with other roles and social purposes of the school such as training for citizenship or the acquisition of a liberal education? What exactly is the role of the school in society? Does it differ greatly from one society to another? Should it?

CHAPTER 5

Educational Curricula and the Nature of Knowledge

Now that we have completed a rough mapping out of the concept 'education', it is important to continue our mapping out of some of the concepts entailed by it. We have observed that education implies knowledge and understanding in breadth and depth; but we said very little about the nature of knowledge nor precisely what constitutes breadth and depth. If we wish to start organizing a program of activities for children designed to bring about their education, then we must be clear about what must go into the program and how it is to be presented. In other words, to build a curriculum for education we must know more about both the nature and types of knowledge as well as about children and how to present knowledge to children. Accordingly in the next two chapters of the book we deal with these topics. In Chapter 5 we will focus on building a curriculum from the perspective of adults, viewing the curriculum as an organization of subject matter drawn from various kinds of knowledge. It is often called the subject-centered approach to curriculum building. In Chapter 6 we focus on the child-centered approach to curriculum construction, an approach which centers on 'needs' and the nature of the child. We shall see that these two approaches are not necessarily in conflict.

The Concept 'Curriculum'

We will begin the discussion by gaining clarity on the concept 'curriculum' itself. A dictionary definition of it will be of little help to us here because public usage of the term has departed widely from it. One dictionary reports that curriculum is 'a course, or a complete set of courses, of a fixed series of prescribed study at a school or college'. Educationalists and curriculum theorists are particularly wide-ranging and often careless in the use of the term. Often nearly everything of educational concern — from teaching methods to philosophical justifications, from course content to evaluation — is placed under the rubric 'curriculum'. There will be no attempt here to map out all the usages. Only a few remarks about curriculum will be made, after which a definition for the discussion will be stipulated.

A few things regarding curriculum are fairly obvious. First, curriculum, as the etymology of the word ('a course, a running') suggests, is a program of activities of a limited sequence engaged in by pupils and teachers for purposes of learning. Secondly, it seems fairly clear that curriculum is institutionally related. My own plan for me to go through a series of activities is not a curriculum. Thirdly, curricula are planned and have purpose. They are not random occurrences and activities. Fourthly, curriculum is a value neutral concept and in this sense is unlike education. This means that one can have a fairly successful curriculum for inculcation of Nazi values, for example, or for making hamburgers. So the first and most important question to ask about curriculum is, 'What is it for?' If it is for education, then a wide range of restrictions, both in content and method, are placed on the program of activities. In our discussion here we will be concerned exclusively with educational curricula, not even those other objectives (see 'The role of school in society' in Chapter 4) of the school worth going after and implementing. So the definition now to be stipulated will reflect that purely educational concern. The definition of educational curriculum used below and throughout this book is one based on the work of Hirst and Peters, thus: a programme of activities engaged in by pupils and teachers designed so that pupils will attain as far as possible certain educational objectives.

Elements of Curriculum

In his *The Logic of Curriculum*,[1] Paul Hirst notes and discusses three important elements to be taken into account in the rational planning of educational curricula. These three elements are: (1) the *method*, or means, for (2) bringing about mastery of *content* (subject matter) for purposes of (3) achieving educational *objectives*, or ends.

Method

Reference to method in curriculum discussions is not necessarily reference to method of teaching, although it certainly also, and perhaps primarily, is that. The method refers to whatever activities students and teachers engage in to accomplish some goals. Thus teachers might instruct, illustrate, display, describe, tell, drill, and so on. Or they might supervise children's activities of play, discovery, lab work, doing exercises, completing 'projects', doing research, and experimenting. The types of activities on the parts of both the teacher and the pupils are almost endless. We already noted in our discussion on the procedural criterion for 'education' that there is very little restriction on methodology; almost anything will count as an educational process or method as long as educational ends are met and the voluntariness of students is not infringed upon. So the question about which methods to use depends primarily on what ends are to be achieved. So unless one knows which content is to be mastered, the choice of methods is irrational. As the proverbial wise man says, 'If you don't know where you're going, any method will get you there'. The selection of method, then, is logically secondary to selection of content.

Content

The content of the curriculum is what was traditionally known as *the* curriculum, a detailed statement of the items of knowledge to be 'covered' or 'taught', sent out to each school by government departments of education. The items of knowledge were grouped under 'subjects' or 'courses' such as geography, chemistry, history and so on. Teachers broke them up into 'units' and 'lessons'. Once the content of the lesson was selected and organized, the teacher could proceed to select a method to teach it (or for students to learn it even if the teacher decided not to teach it directly). Traditionally, rational planning began with content, at least for the teacher in the classroom. It is a merit in Hirst's discussion on curriculum to propose that rational curriculum planning begins even earlier than that. For content, too, is selected only as means to bring about further educational ends. When utilitarian considerations for purposes of schools are put aside, the selection of content for educational reasons becomes central to the planning. The content of an educational curriculum is selected to bring about those valuable qualities of mind characteristic of the educated person. When literature is selected as developing understanding of mankind's aesthetic experience and insight into the unique nature of man, the content selected and the method of teaching are different than when literature is seen as an exercise in reading and a preparation for employment. When chemistry is viewed as developing scientific understanding rather than preparation for pharmacy or nursing, then content and method shift accordingly. Rational planning for educational curricula begins with consideration of those qualities of mind that are required for a well-rounded complete education.

Objectives

The end, or objective, of education, for which there is no further goal, is a fully developed mind and, correspondingly, the fully developed person. Those 'forms of knowledge', or 'modes of experience', or 'forms of rationality' (all interchangeable phrases for Hirst and Peters) are the seven 'forms' already referred to. These do not represent 'disciplines' or 'courses' or 'subject'. They are the logical types of knowledge and rationality out of which subjects and courses are built. Sometimes a course partakes of several forms. Geography represents aspects of the forms of logic, empirical science, human sciences, and even ethics. Sometimes there are several courses within one 'form'. Biology, chemistry, and physics are all in the 'form' called empirical science. The precise nature of the forms will be discussed below in the section on 'The differentiation of knowledge'. An educational curriculum will comply with the demand for breadth of knowledge as well as depth. Content that initiates everyone into all the 'forms' will be required for educational breadth to be satisfied. The question of depth is satisfied in part by making sure that justification for making knowledge claims is fully satisfied. To understand this fully we need to look more closely at the nature of knowledge itself.

The Nature of Knowledge

Knowledge-That and Education

What, then, is knowledge? The answer depends in part on the kinds of things known. Knowing how to ride a bicycle is a very different kind of achievement from knowing that New York is a large city. The objects of knowledge are many and corresponding objects of learning are likewise many. If we listed all the typical kinds of things that can be known we might come up with a list of 'A knows X' where X is:

1 a person, place, or thing. A knows Vancouver.
2 knowledge how. A knows how to ride a bicycle.
3 knowledge that. A knows that the cat is on the mat.
4 knowledge what. A knows what causes the rain to fall.
5 knowledge who. A knows who won the game.
6 knowledge about. A knows about cars.
7 knowledge of the way. A knows the way to town.
8 knowledge how to be. A knows how to be faithful.

The list could probably go on. What is to be noted is that all the x's can be reduced either to knowing-how or to knowing-that. When, for example, I say 'I know *who* won the game', I can without change in meaning say 'I know *that* the game was won by y'. For 'I know the *way*...' I can substitute, 'I know *that* the way to...', etc. The theory of the reducibility of all knowledge to 'how' and 'that' is not without controversy. Some would like to reduce all knowledge to 'how', others, all knowledge to 'that'. Still others think the two classes are not exhaustive, and that knowledge of persons, for example, is a separate category. The details of these arguments, though interesting, are not taken up here. It is, however, fair to say that the irreducibility of two kinds of knowledge to 'how' and 'that' is widely accepted, and that in any case they constitute the main types of knowledge.

More controversial is the claim, which will here be considered acceptable, that the main kind of knowledge for educational purposes is knowledge-that, which will be identified as propositional knowledge. This is already largely implied by the 'understanding' requirement attached to the knowledge condition for education. Understanding just is not the sort of thing that is necessary for knowing how to ride a bicycle. If one did have understanding of, say, the principles of physics according to which momentum and balance were a function of each other, that knowledge would be over and above knowing-how and could be reduced to propositions. The same might be said for the skills of knowing how to read and how to compute, where the elements of understanding are reducible to propositions. In many other areas of school learning where the knowledge is merely technique of how to do things, this might qualify as training, but not as education. That which renders certain kinds of learning educational is the acquistion of propositional knowledge.

Conditions of Knowledge-That

Theory of knowledge, or epistemology, is one of the main branches of the discipline of philosophy; and it is concerned in large part with the necessary and sufficient conditions for correctly claiming to know that something is the case. As early as Plato, philosophy pondered over questions about such things as the distinction between believing x and knowing x; or between knowing and having true belief; or about what can be known with certainty; or what was the nature of reality which can be known, and so on. It is not the object of this course to delve deeply into these interesting questions. What is possible to do here is to submit for consideration three conditions which are accepted by and large (with variation) by philosophers as necessary and sufficient for knowing. These conditions are: (1) belief, (2) truth, and (3) evidence.

Belief

What is meant by saying that belief is a necessary condition for knowing propositions is that one must be aware, or have been aware (one cannot be aware when one is asleep), of having entertained the proposition as true. 'Having entertained the proposition as true' is about as close to the notion of belief as one can come without making matters complicated. People are sometimes confused by this condition because they have been taught that believing and knowing are very different states of mind; and so they are. But it is not being claimed that believing is sufficient for claiming to know; only that it is necessary. *Merely* believing is never sufficient for knowing.

What also is not meant by positing this condition for knowing is the commitment sense of 'believing', as when religious people believe *in* something or somebody. Indeed, as will be pointed out further below, matters of belief or faith without further conditions being met cannot be considered curriculum candidates because they are not forms of *knowledge*, where knowledge requires evidence for propositions to be believed.

The belief condition is sometimes challenged by citing alleged examples of knowing where no belief is present, as when a bereaved lover is presented with the undisputable proof that his love has deceased and yet he claims. 'I don't believe it!' Such a person is said to know without believing. However, the fact is that either he believes but will not admit to it or he does not know but merely has the other two conditions of knowing satisfied, namely the truth and evidence conditions.

Truth

The truth condition for knowing is simply that that which is claimed in the proposition which is known is in fact the case. By 'truth' is meant simply 'What is the case' or 'that which is so'. And the condition asserts that it is logically impossible for anyone to know any proposition which is not true. There are, of course, many instances in which people *do* claim to know something that, it later turns out, is not true. 'The earth is flat' is a proposition once thought to be true, and the evidence *seemed* to suggest this. But it cannot be said that people once upon a time *knew* that the earth was flat before the evidence came in to prove otherwise. Knowledge claims, in other words, are defeasible; they can be undone and made void when it is found out the truth ran counter to the claim. Skeptics who find the truth condition too stringent often remark that since every proposition is subject to correction it therefore follows that we can know nothing. The next step in their argument is that since we obviously do know at least a few things, it therefore must be the case that the truth condition does not apply for instances of knowing. Is such an argument satisfactory? No. It does not follow that since every proposition is *subject* to correction we therefore can know nothing. Some propositions, though subject to correction, are correct. We are justified in claiming to know them. Perhaps the only merit in the skeptic's argument is to make us more cautious about what we are entitled to claim to know. The entitlement comes from the satisfaction of the evidence condition.

Evidence

It is not sufficient for someone who believes a true proposition to claim to know it. In addition to the belief and truth conditions it is also necessary to have evidence, to be able to cite the grounds for believing the propositions to be true. This condition is also referred to as the justification condition, meaning by that that when one says 'I know...' one has earned the right to make that claim on the grounds that adequate relevant evidence is publicly available to anyone who puts himself into a position to assess it and that the claimant has already assessed it.

When sufficient evidence for the truth of a proposition is ascertained then one is entitled, or justified, in claiming to know the

Figure 1: Propositional knowledge

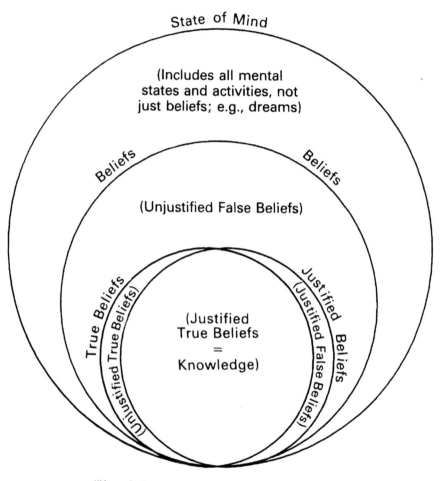

State of Mind

(Includes all mental
states and activities, not
just beliefs; e.g., dreams)

Beliefs

Beliefs

(Unjustified False Beliefs)

True Beliefs

(Unjustified True Beliefs)

Justified Beliefs

(Justified False Beliefs)

(Justified
True Beliefs
=
Knowledge)

"Knowledge-that" ≅ df. "justified, true, belief."

N.B. This diagram does not capture the important fact that truth
is *not* a state of mind. The condition for something being
true is external to mind.

proposition. This is so even if the proposition is in fact false, as determined by later and still further evidence. This means that sometimes a justified belief can be false. If that is the case, then one simply withdraws the claim and admits being in error, even if justifiably in error. This again points to the need for caution in making knowledge claims. (For further clarification see Figure 1.)

Attacks on the evidence condition often take the form of noting the conviction with which people make claims to know when no evidence is at hand. Such people *seem* 'to know' by intuition or imaginative leaps. Thus sports fans say, 'I knew the Lions would win', when of course they didn't know because they only hoped and wanted them to win or had a feeling they just might 'do the impossible'. Or the jealous wife 'knew by intuition' the moment her husband came in that he 'had been up to something'; which he had been, but which the wife did not 'know' because she had no evidence. Nothing she 'knew' would hold up in any court if it came to that.

Though intuition is not one type of evidence for knowing, there are indeed a number of other and different ways of knowing, each one being so distinct that one can determine the logical types of knowing on the basis of the several distinctive types of truth tests. Paul Hirst, who has developed a theory of forms of knowledge (already commented on in Chapters 3 and 4 and in the section on 'Objectives') uses the evidence condition, or the truth test, as the major criterion for selecting a 'form' or knowledge. Since these 'forms' play a central role in selection of educational curriculum objectives it is important to be clear about what constitutes a 'form' and precisely what these forms are.

The Differentiation of Knowledge

The bases on which knowledge is differentiated, and which for Hirst constitutes the criteria for picking out 'forms of knowledge', are several, but two are clearly central. First, a form of knowledge has a distinctive truth test, as just noted above. To satisfy the evidence condition for knowing, the truth of a proposition must be adequately tested according to the canons of a particular form. In the empirical sciences, whatever else they require, a true proposition must ultimately satisfy the test of sense experience. In logical claims that is irrelevant, but satisfying rules of transformation from premise to conclusion is a must. The two 'forms', empirical science and logic,

Table 1: Forms of knowledge (Hirst's analysis)

Forms:	Characterized by: Central Concepts	Distinctive Truth Tests	Methodology of Investigation
1 *Pure Mathematics and Logic*	integer, matrix, number, presupposition, inference, deduction, consistency	validity of deduction and inference	— syllogistic deduction — logical rules (e.g. non-contradiction) — necessary and sufficient conditions for use of a term
2 *Physical (empirical) Sciences*	cause-effect, gravity, motion, force, time, substance	— matching sense experience — empirical data	— observation — experimentation — control situations
3 *History and Human Sciences*	— unique events — reason — cause continuum — mental terms (wanting, hoping, doing, deciding, ambition) — purpose, will	sense experience *plus* understanding of the human element — reasons for doing, acting, striving	— observation (of records) — re-creation of human events in imagination — interpreting reasons for acting

4 *Aesthetics*	— harmony, beauty, nice, gorgeous, elegant, rhythm, grace, style, melody, counter point	— various — form recognition e.g., literature — theme universality, style, imagery, rhythm, truth	— listening — feeling — intuiting — observing — imagining
5 *Morals*	— ought, good, bad, right, wrong, wicked, honourable	— 'good' reasons based on presupposed fundamental principles such as honesty, justice, respect, freedom, consideration of interests	— practical syllogism — grounding reasons for action on principles — checking against experience
6 *Philosophy*	— meaning, sense, assumption, metaphysics, justification, second order	— consistency — validity of argument — proper inference — clarity of meaning	— logical rules — paradigm case — deduction — necessary and sufficient conditions for meaning of x (criteria) — unearthing assumptions
7 *Religion*	God, sin, transcendant, Nirvana, redemption, spiritual, awe	revelation? authority? analogical inference	— check against sacred books and authorities — philosophical argument

are thus distinctive types. As we shall see, there are also others. The second criterion asserts that there are a number of central concepts within a form which are key notions in that form and exclusively in that form. The concepts 'duty' and 'wicked' are moral concepts; 'beauty' and 'harmony', aesthetic concepts. A third criterion, which is sometimes listed as a separate one and sometimes as a part of the second one, is that the central concepts are all inter-related. Thus 'wicked' is the result of and/or reason for not doing one's 'duty'; 'harmony' is one characteristic of objects of art which produces 'beauty'; 'cause' and 'effect' function in tandem; 'intention' and 'action' are inter-related; and so on. Another, and fourth, criterion is included in Hirst's writings. Reference is to the distinctive methodology of investigation for each form. Such a criterion is, however, not a matter of a logical condition for a 'form', but an empirical claim about how people operate. The criterion is perhaps and at best an easy way, though not a foolproof way, of deciding in which form a person is investigating. A person gazing into a test-tube is not likely to be a philosopher; nor is one with feet on the desk gazing out of the window a scientist. In Table 1, the method of investigation is included for your consideration. The diagram represents in brief form Hirst's widely known and discussed theory of the forms of knowledge.

A few words of explanation for the Table are appropriate. First, it should be noted that the order of naming the forms in the left column is relatively arbitrary, and is not Hirst's order. The order, however, is not entirely arbitrary for an attempt has been made to list them in order of the clarity and universal acceptability. Forms (1) and (2), for example, are universally acknowledged. Form (7) on the other hand is often denied entirely as a form of knowledge. The double line between forms (5) and (6) represents your author's cut-off point, form (6) being in doubt not because there is no philosophical knowledge but because it seems arguable that this form could be collapsed into form (1). Whether or not philosophy is a branch of logic is a legitimate concern, but is too technical for consideration here. It should further be noted that the list is intended to be exhaustive and represents *all* extant logical types of knowledge so far developed by mankind. And so it follows that this list also exhausts the possibilities for curriculum inclusion. It does not follow, however, that subjects, courses, and curriculum units must adhere to purity of form. How to arrange curriculum details around topics, courses, or even lessons is a further and separate concern. It does not follow, for example, that just because ethical knowledge is part of being educated that lessons or courses in ethics must be presented. Perhaps, although this needs to be shown on good empirical evidence, the best way to achieve moral understanding is through example and periodical discussions within contexts of day-to-day living and within other lessons. Such practical questions, though interesting and important, are not philosophical and will not be dealt with here further.

Criticism of Hirst's 'Forms of Knowledge'

Some points of criticism about Hirst's 'forms of knowledge' theory are now discussed. First, it is not all that obvious that all the forms are forms of *knowledge*. If, as has been argued, knowledge is justified true belief, then it would appear that at least some forms are not *knowledge* because the truth of the statements made cannot even in principle be justified. There seems little doubt that scientific statements, which are based on sense experience, and logical and mathematical statements, based on reason, are acceptable as truth yielding. In fact it has been held by some philosophers (the logical positivists) that science and logic are the *only* forms of truth test. But what can be said about the other forms (forms 3 to 7 in Table 1) regarding the application of the term 'true' to statements made in those categories? Negatively we can say that statements made in them are not based on authority, not based on wide appeal and majority opinion, and not based on private experience.[2] Statements, if they are genuine knowledge claims, must satisfy public, intersubjective canons of verifiability. To find out what these canons are in each form would require lengthy studies in the philosophy of each form, for which this is not the occasion. A study of the philosophy of history, for example, would reveal that historical statements are verified not *merely* by citing sense experience, though it is *in part* that, but also citing the motives, intentions, hopes, and fears of a people whose existence is imaginatively re-created and re-constituted according to their perspective in their time. The evidence historians submit for this reconstruction is not the same as scientists submit for their statements; but it is evidence, evidence which yields historical truth. In like manner different kinds of evidence are appropriate to statements made in ethics, in aesthetics, and in philosophy. There remains a serious difficulty with religious propositions and the test for their truth. The most serious charge against a religious form of knowledge is that religious statements do not even make sense, since there is not even a *conceivable* way of testing them. The less serious claim is that they do make sense but cannot in fact be verified and so the term *true* does not apply to them. This view seems to be reflected in the public school climate in our day, for religion is not taught as though its propositions are true. If there is a mention of religion it is usually in the form of true statements *about* religion. The latter is not religious education in the true sense of the term, however. For religious education to be logically possible, where 'education' is used in the E_3 sense noted, it would have to be the case that religious knowledge is possible. And we have just proposed that such knowledge is not possible. If that is so, then there remain only six Hirstian 'forms' as candidates for curriculum construction.

A second problem with Hirst's forms concerns the direct applicability of these forms for purposes of curriculum construction. Theorists and teachers interested in self-expression for children, in creativity, in inter-disciplinary or integrated education, in child-centered rather than subject-centered education, are unimpressed with Hirst's forms even if they can be seen as correct and complete. In general, the objection to Hirst is similar to the objection against Peters' analysis of education (see section on 'Intellectualism' in chapter 3), that it is too intellectual and congnitive and not sufficiently concerned with emotion and the 'affective' domain of human concern. The worry is whether those concerned with emotional and perceptual experiences and with skill performance in students can reconcile that concern with Hirst's knowledge forms. There is, however, no need to worry for knowing, doing, and feeling are very closely inter-related. Furthermore, Hirst's concern is with 'liberal education', where the affective and the conative are central to educational concerns. Here, as noted with respect to the charge of intellectualism against Peters (see Chapter 3), the cognitive and the affective are fundamentally intertwined. We do not, for example, feel guilt if we have no knowledge of what it is wrong to do. Such arguments showing the inter-relatedness of feeling and knowing, do not, however, settle the matter about how to teach, about whether a curriculum should be exclusively concerned with facts or whether children's interests should not be considered. We will return to such considerations in the next chapter. The point to be made here is that it is not inherent in Hirst's theory that a particular form of teaching and/or curriculum approach be adopted. Nor clearly is Hirst recommending a curriculum objective only for the very highly academically able. He clearly regards forms of knowledge as suitable and necessary for all students.

There are a number of more technical problems concerning Hirst's forms which will be only briefly referred to here. One such problem is whether artistic statements are actually statements about art, in which case they would be philosophical, or whether the work of art itself is the statement. Usually it is thought Hirst meant the latter. But in what sense is a painting or a piece of music a statement? There is, in other words, a point of controversy about how to view and to verify as true, artistic statements. Another problem concerns the inter-relationship between the forms. To what extent are the forms really distinct if they rely on one another? Can some forms in fact be collapsed into others? And with respect to logic (form 1 in the Table), how is a mathematical statement verified by a 'test against experience', which is demanded by Hirst as a condition for there being a form.

Despite these and other problems in the 'forms of knowledge' thesis, it does nevertheless stand out as the major attempt to map the domain of propositional knowledge into logical types which can become candidates for consideration in curriculum construction. We shall, therefore, continue to refer to six forms of knowledge (Hirst's seven, minus religion) representing the complete circle of knowledge into which initiation is required for one to be considered educated.

As we turn next to a consideration of curriculum construction from the perspective of the child, that is, child-centered rather than subject-centered curricula, we will find that the so-called 'progressive' movement in education no less than the more 'traditional' approach to education relies on some unexpressed views about necessary modes of knowledge and experience. In fact Hirst and Peters, in their *Logic of Education*, deem the 'forms of knowledge' thesis to be the underlying reconciliation between the apparently diverse 'authoritarian' and 'child-centered' approaches to education.[3]

Suggested further readings:

HIRST, P.H. and PETERS, R.S. (1970) *op. cit.*, pp. 60–73.

HIRST P.H. (1969) 'The logic of the curriculum' in *Journal of Curriculum Studies*.

HIRST, P.H. (1974) *Knowledge and the Curriculum*, London, Routledge and Kegan Paul.

LLOYD, D.I. (1976) 'Knowledge and education' and WRINGE, D.S. (1976) 'Forms of knowledge', in LLOYD D.I. (Ed.) *Philosophy and the Teacher*, London, Routledge and Kegan Paul, ch. 5 and 6.

Notes

1   HIRST, P.H. (1969) 'The logic of the curriculum' *Journal of Curriculum Studies.*
2   See in this connection LLOYD, D.I. (Ed.) (1976) *Philosophy and the Teacher*, London Routledge and Kegan Paul, pp. 66 and 67.
3   See their 'Introduction' to that work.

Questions and Exercises

Briefly answer the following questions:
1   Is 'curriculum' a value term like 'education' is? Explain.
2   In curriculum planning what is the logical priority of the following three components: content, method, objective?
3   In education which is more important knowledge-how or knowledge-that? Explain.
4   What does it mean to say that knowledge claims are defeasible?
5   Can there be justified false beliefs?
6   What conditions must be satisfied for us to claim to know a proposition?
7   Why could the following statement not be considered a case of knowledge 'You see, I was right; she was at home. I knew it because I could feel it in my bones.'
8   It is essential to our concept of 'knowledge' that evidence be public. Does this requirement present a problem for the idea of 'religious knowledge'?

Answer the following:
1   In *The Logic of Education*, pp. 62, 63, Hirst and Peters state that: 'it is only through the mastery of a body of public concepts, with their related objective tests, that objective experience and knowledge can be achieved.' What are these 'modes' or 'forms' of knowledge and experience? List them. What are their distinctive truth tests? State them. Do you see any problems with one or more of these 'forms of knowledge'?
2   Which of the following statements belong to which 'form' or 'mode' of knowledge and experience?

    (a)   You have an obligation to return that book.
    (b)   That conclusion does not follow from the previous statements.
    (c)   She moves so gracefully.
    (d)   If you want to get to the airport in a hurry you should take a taxi.

(e) The internal angles of a triangle equal 180 degrees.
(f) You should help someone in need.
(g) God created the universe.
(h) Revenge was their main reason for going to war.
(i) The building was constructed very well.
(j) Knowledge is justified true belief.

3   Explain the statement 'knowledge is justified true belief, and show why it is important for educators to be aware of it in curriculum construction.

CHAPTER 6

Child-Centered Curricula

Contrasting Approaches to Curriculum

In the last chapter we considered some philosophical issues in curriculum from the perspective of an adult interested in providing valuable knowledge for children. That perspective, focusing as it does on curriculum content, is often referred to as the traditional subject-centered curriculum approach. As we have already briefly noted earlier and as we shall see further below, the approach as presented in the last Chapter is scarcely traditional although it is 'subject' centered in some respects. In contrast to such a view, it is often claimed, with alleged support from moral and psychological authority, that curriculum considerations should proceed from the perspective of the child. One of the central ideas in child-centered education is to start from the child. The two starting points, the subject on the one hand and the child on the other hand, lead to two broadly contrasting approaches to education generally, which in the politics of education have been referred to as the 'traditional' and the 'progressive' approaches. These two approaches have led to much unnecessary animosity and divisiveness in education because each 'side' unfairly caricatures the other at an unwarranted extreme. A good teacher carefully adopts elements of both positions. It is instructive, nevertheless, to examine these two approaches for their strengths and weaknesses.[1]

A cluster of notions have, for better or worse, attached themselves to 'traditional' education. Some of these are: subject-centered, intellect, standards, lessons, examination, structure, work and discipline, teaching, obedience, mastery of subject content, memory work, order, accountability, control and other related concepts. Similarly a cluster of notions have attached themselves to 'progressive' education. Some of these are: child-centered, emotion, activity, utility and relevance, discovery, understanding concepts, critical thinking, process, freedom, facilitation of learning, experience, growth, creativity, problem-centered and other related concepts. Good thought and good practice in education requires adoption of ideas from both approaches. To illustrate how inter-dependent the two approaches are, consider the two slogans, 'We teach subjects' and 'We teach children' taken respectively from 'traditional' and 'progressive' stances. Clearly these two ideas require each other, for subjects are not taught unless they are taught to someone and one just cannot teach someone without teaching them something. Consider also the impossibility of being creative without requisite skills and knowledge which make creativeness possible. Nor is it possible to think critically unless one has mastered some information about which to be critical. And the ideas of freedom and authority are also not incompatible. Being *an* authority (on subject matter and teaching methods) and being *in* authority (in the role of teacher which carries with it certain rights and responsibilities) does not mean that one must be *authoritarian* (dominating and threatening from a position of power). Legitimate authority and legitimate freedom are compatible. The two approaches in their extreme form are not in fact educationally feasible. It is a merit in the Hirst and Peters' 'forms of knowledge' thesis that in it the two opposing approaches can be reconciled, for both 'traditional' and 'progressive' educators can without surrendering the strengths in their respective positions adopt as the ultimate curriculum objective the achievement of those forms of knowledge and experience so necessary for the full development of the person.

Some 'progressive' educators would, however, object even to this. They would claim that to choose objectives for a child in any form is wrong, for it is to make value judgments about what is good for children. Instead they advocate again 'starting from the child' by studying children to see what their needs are, and thus by meeting those needs avoid making that value judgment and at the same time place education on a sound scientific foundation. There are, however, several problems in holding to such a position. First, the moral stance taken is based on a fallacy. The stance that 'one must not make judgments of value for others' is based on a prior moral notion of freedom, namely, 'that each person should be free to choose his own values'. The latter, however, can apply only to those who have the insight and requisite knowledge to make intelligent choice; so it cannot apply to the very young and only somewhat to those of of partial maturity. The fallacy, then, is to invoke a principle of ethics in the wrong setting, to the wrong people at the wrong time. Secondly, the position taken is self-defeating. To tell others that they must not tell others what to do is to tell others what to do. That is a cryptic way of saying that there can be no escape from taking a value position in education. The important issue is to make well-justified and open value decisions so the positions can be scrutinized publicly. The third problem is that the notion of meeting children's needs is not entirely a scientific matter. As our further examination of the 'needs' doctrine will show, the concept 'needs' is a hybrid moral/scientific notion. Appeal to it does not render educational judgments value-neutral. For these reasons, and to illustrate in detail how easily one can err by adopting empty slogans in the name of innovation and progress, we shall now make a close examination of the 'needs' curriculum.

The 'Needs' Curriculum

It is tempting for educators who wish to recommend one type of school programme over others to avoid the inherent questions of value by ignoring them. Instead of bringing arguments and evidence to bear on a discussion about the worth and soundness of their recommendations, they couch their prescriptions in pseudo-technical language. Appeals are made to the facts of 'children's needs' or 'human nature' in order to justify the rightness of a programme and to close off further discussion. If there is any disagreement, we are told, it is simply because we are ignorant of the relevant facts. Thus a problem of value is transformed into an empirical question, 'so that problems of the curriculum and of learning, which have been somewhat intractable and centres of dispute in the past, can now be handed over to the sociologist or the psychologist for definitive solution'.[2]

The Concept 'Need'

A careful analysis of the concept of 'need', however, shows that the concept is itself not value-free, and therefore cannot be called upon as a neutral judge to settle the issues of curriculum content. One of the most obvious conditions of someone being in need is that there exists a norm or standard which ought to be satisfied. 'Need' statements are therefore norm statements. To say that a family needs x amount of income is to say that they ought not to have less than a certain amount considered the accepted standard. Such a standard is a judgment of value. Even to say that a child needs food is to appeal to the value judgment that children ought not to die of starvation. Value judgments cannot be avoided in need statements. At the same time, however, there is an appeal in the 'need' statement to certain facts in the case. The second condition for being in 'need', then, is that the norm in fact has not been reached or may well fail to be reached. To say that a child needs food is to say that the child in fact has little or no food, or it is to say that if the food he has is taken away he will in fact suffer consequences he should not suffer. In this way the concept 'need' is a hybrid value/scientific statement. The value cannot be empirically determined; the facts in the case must be empirically determined.

Another aspect of the concept 'need' is that the thing that is said to be needed must measure up to the norm or standard implied. If it is food that is needed, then nutrients must be provided; toys and love will not do. If attention is needed, food will not do. And so on. This condition, mentioned by Dearden alongside the other two conditions noted above, is a point well taken, but may well be an important fact about needs rather than a logical condition for the meaning of 'needs'. Be that as it may, what about the use of the term 'needs' in educational curricula? '

'Needs' in Educational Curricula

Given that 'need' statements are statements about norms and the absence of those norms, is it the case that we should build a curriculum by satisfying the educational needs of children? Is one, in other words, justified in basing the curriculum on the needs of children? The answer is quite obviously, yes. But one should note how empty the suggestion is. If 'needs' are 'ought' statements, then the question could just as well read, 'Ought we to provide children with a curriculum which they ought to have?' Clearly we ought to; but the suggestion is otiose. More to the point are questions such as: What ought the standards to be? What *are* the children's educational needs? How, and on what grounds, will these be determined? Does one examine students to determine what standards they ought to achieve? What can one learn from Johnny about what Johnny needs? Under normal circumstances there is nothing within Johnny that will determine whether or not he ought to learn Algebra, Shakespeare, or French. These are thought to be worthwhile things for Johnny to achieve, given certain values placed on knowledge and on societal demands. However, once the standards are in place, then clearly Johnny can be examined to see if he has reached these standards. If not, then he will still need to learn the requisite things. Empirical information about Johnny's state of ignorance or knowledge is not beside the point; but it also is not the only crucial point. What he *ought* to achieve, given his at least normal ability, given the value of certain forms of knowledge and understanding, and given certain social demands, is the central question in determination of the educational curriculum he should follow.

Non-Educational Needs and the School

What are Johnny's *educational* needs is of course a very different question from what other needs he may have, some of which the school can and perhaps should satisfy. A number of different types of needs can be distinguished. *Biological* needs, such as for food, shelter, rest and so on are not the sort of needs a school usually caters to. On occasion schools are involved in satisfying these. Sometimes lunches or other foods are served; more often mass health concerns such as eye and ear testing, vaccinations, or safety regulations are handled under school auspices. *Psychological* needs, such as for love and security, are also usually catered to outside the schools, though of course there is no logical reason why they should not also be in part the concern of the school. Two types of *functional* needs are of considerable concern in the school. One such set of needs concerns the standards set in the community according to which children are eventually expected to conform. Some of these standards — say, standards of dress, decorum, inter-personal relations, and so on — are fairly common to all and are sometimes referred to as basic needs. Other standards vary from individual to individual, depending on role and occupation in society. It is a reasonable demand to expect the school to cater to some extent to these needs. And it is certainly a legitimate expectation that the school satisfy those other functional needs that can be considered the immediate pre-conditions for obtaining an education. Central among these are the need to read and write (and perhaps these days to use computers), the need to do elementary mathematics, the need to be provided with essential learning materials, and the need for a suitable learning environment, which includes some psychological and bio-logical needs.

All such non-educational needs, while they do appeal to an agreed upon value (usually), are determined by and large on empir-ical grounds. But when it comes to setting the standards for achieve-ment in knowledge and understanding (in other words, standards of education) the value question looms large again, for here there is more disagreement. Here simple appeal to 'needs' gets us nowhere. Arguments will need to be mounted to show why particular knowl-edge is deemed to be valuable and so becomes a candidate for inclusion in the curriculum. One such brief argument will be made later in this chapter and again in Chapter 10, where the justification of education will be considered. But before we consider such an argument here, we want to consider needs in connection with motivation.

'Needs' and Motivation

It is sometimes held that appeal to children's needs will solve the problem of motivation in education. The problem intended to be solved is that of getting children to be more attentive to and more interested in what they should be learning and as a result learn more, and more efficiently. The assumption is that children learn more and better if they learn what they *want* to learn. On the assumption that that assumption is warranted (although even that needs examination), the appeal to needs will work only if what the child needs (ought to have) is identical with what he wants, which could be called his 'felt needs'. But if the 'felt needs' are identical to the actual needs then there is no motivational problem. And if the actual needs of the child (say to learn his times table) are at odds with the child's wants or 'felt needs' (say, to go out and play) then the teacher's appeal to the 'felt needs', will not solve the problem of getting the child interested in and attentive to his times table. In other words, the appeal to needs to solve the motivational problem will not work in any event. Nor does it help to shift the language to that of interests. It is sometimes said that we could solve the motiva-tional problem by appealing to children's interests; but the same sort of difficulty arises. If children are *interested in* what is *in their interest* (and that is equivalent to being interested in what ought to be learnt) then there is no motivational problem. But if there is no interest in doing what is in their interest, then appeal to their present interests will not help. Formally stated, these points can now be summarized as follows:

1 'x wants y' does not entail 'x needs y', and 'x does not want y' does not entail 'x does not need y'
2 'x is interested in y' does not entail 'y is in the interest of x', and 'x is not interested in y' does not entail 'y is not in the interest of x.'

These same points are made in Figure 2.

Figure 2: Needs, wants, and interests in education

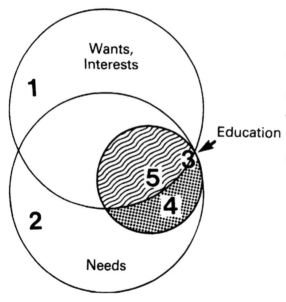

1. Wants, interests ('felt' needs)

2. Needs (of all kinds); what is in one's interest.

3. Educational needs

4. Spotted area is area of motivational problem in education.

5. Lined area is area of education in which children want what they need; are interested in what is in their interest; there is no motivational problem.

Human Nature Considerations

We have observed in the last section that escape from the value issues in education cannot be achieved by appeal to the needs of children. In this section we will see that appeal to human nature also is no escape from value judgments in education and that the child-centered movement takes a very ill-considered view about the significance of human nature in the planning of educational curricula. Human nature assumptions underpin many child-centered theories of education including key notions such as growth, open-education, individualized instruction, self-education, values clarification, as well as the needs doctrine. With respect to needs, it is felt that somehow what the child really needs is already written into its nature. No doubt all educational theories subscribe to, or at least make implicit assumptions about, some theory of human nature. So it is important by all accounts to be clear about the role human nature plays in educational theory. There are three questions that we will consider: (1) What is the meaning of 'human nature'? (2) What in fact are some true statements about human nature? (3) What is the significance of human nature statements in education? We will begin by examining the concept itself.

The Concept 'Human Nature'

When we ask, 'What is human nature?' we are not in the first instance asking for predication of facts about human nature but about its meaning. So what does the term mean? It means, first, that reference is being made to a property or quality of human beings that is unique to human beings. *Uniqueness* to the species is, then, one condition for referring to a quality as one of human nature. We do not say, for example, that having blood is part of *human* nature, because we share that with all animals, although it would be correct to say that it is part of our animal nature. However, when we ask for the nature of something we are asking for its distinguishing features, for that which sets it apart from all other things. A second condition is that the distinguishing feature be a property that is universal to the species. *Universality* to the species is required for some properly to be referred to as part of our human nature. The ability to learn to speak a language is part of human nature, but speaking English is not. Fear of falling, if psychology correctly informs us, is part of human nature; fear of snakes is not, because the latter is not universal. Another reason fear of snakes is not part of human nature is that the fear has been learnt. Part of the meaning of human nature is that the properly so referred to is *non-acquired.* We are born with those properties that are correctly described as part of our nature. The reason fear of falling is said to be part of our nature is that it is an instinct within all of us at birth. Still another reason fear of falling is said to be part of our nature is that the fear is persistent. It is very difficult, if not impossible, to overcome such fear and to be trained not to fear. *Persistency* is, then, yet another condition for calling some attribute part of our nature. And there is still another condition, *significance.* Even if a particular characteristic fulfills all the other conditions, it is not usually referred to as part of our nature unless it makes an important difference, unless it strikes at the heart and essence of our being. Aristotle once noted that man was the only featherless biped. The temptation is to reply, 'so what?' And what if we did have six rather than five fingers on each hand? It is hard to imagine that that would be significant and thus be pinpointed as part of our human nature. But our having thumbs and thus the ability to create things is very much more likely to be considered part of our nature because the attribute makes a significant difference to us as a species. The above conditions taken together allow us to summarize as follows: human nature is the term used to refer to those attributes of human beings which are unique to the species, universal, non-acquired, persistent, and significant.

The Description of Human Nature

When it comes to naming the attributes of human beings that are referred to as their nature according to the conditions just mentioned, we run into considerable difficulty. Such description, it should be noted, is not typically a task for philosophers, for we are dealing with factual rather than conceptual or logical matters. Perhaps some features of human nature are best described by social scientists such as psychologists and anthropologists. They at least attempt to isolate some features of human beings that are universal. But, as we now know, that is not a sufficient condition for selecting features to be described as human nature. The general problem is that too few researchers have systematically studied human beings from a perspective using the criteria outlined in the last section. Furthermore, it may even be impossible to do so, since when we study human beings we study them in the context of their culture, which is an acquired set of human achievements. A psychologist studying children at birth from many different races and locations would be as close as one could come to getting some reliable information. Sociologists and anthropologists studying 'primitive' peoples may provide some information, though the information would probably be 'tainted' with culturally acquired characteristics. The small amount of reliable information available suggests that human beings have by nature very few instincts, such as fear of falling, and a few primary drives, such as sucking instinct, hunger, aversion to pain, and sexuality, all of which we share with animals. There is also some evidence that we have a native acquisitiveness and a sense of territoriality. We want to possess things and have a space of our own. But there is very little more that one can cite at this primary level. At the level of 'cultural universals' it has been said that man is a rational animal, a political animal, a symbolizing animal, a religious (spiritual) animal, a social animal, and an artistic (creative) animal. These are, of course, achievements within a culture. What is universal, unique, non-acquired, persistent, and significant about such observations is that man has the *potential* for these things. Human nature, then, is primarily one vast potential for becoming what others design for one to become *and* what one designs for oneself to become. The best way to study what potential consists of is to study those things which mankind has already done and accomplished. So the best way to study 'human nature' is to study history. What in fact is being argued here is that mankind has really only an *animal* nature. That which is *human* about human nature is not natural. It is a cultural over-lay on the animal nature; it is an extraordinary act of achievement in our collective history. Such a view has been nicely expressed by Oakeshott. He says:

> Human beings are what they understand themselves to be
> . . .man is what he becomes; he has a history but no nature.[3]

The human achievement is primarily the achievement of language and rationality, and also, as a result of that, achievement in the other 'cultural universals' already referred to. If what has been argued to this point regarding education is correct, then it can be confidently said that education, because it represents achievement in various forms of rationality, is the route of fulfilling our human nature. Democritus long ago said:

> Nature and teaching are similar, for teaching transforms men, and as it transforms them, it creates nature.[4]

The main useful description of human nature, then, is that mankind is fluid, malleable, full of potential. How man fulfills that potential depends to a large extent on his educational decisions, particularly decisions about curriculum content. What kind of decisions we make in education cannot depend on what our human nature is; for what kind of human beings we become depends on the decisions we make. Of what significance then is a study of human nature? To that question we now turn.

Human Nature Considerations in Education

The value of studying human nature for purposes of education might well be questioned. We have already observed in the last section that there is very little specific guidance one can get from observing that mankind has a great deal of potential; and to understand the kind of potential people have, one studies history, not human nature. We observed also that there is very little information available about basic instincts and drives that go beyond the animal level. Added to these observations we can reiterate the point made in Chapter 2 regarding the naturalistic fallacy. The point made, and worth repeating, is that it is a logical mistake to attempt to derive an *ought* (What *ought* one to include in the curriculum?) from an *is* (What *is* the case with respect to the nature of these children?). If, for example, we found that we all were by nature acquisitive, or even greedy, would we for that reason build an educational programme to enhance those qualities? Hardly. In other words, even if we could describe human nature in some detail, this would give us no guidance about what we ought to place in the curriculum. So it appears that human nature considerations can be, and perhaps should be, disregarded in educational decision-making. But that position states the case too strongly. All that follows so far is that the major decisions about curriculum content, about the forms of rationality to develop in children, are not deducible from human nature considerations.

There are, however, some judgments in education that can be made on the basis of human nature considerations. While human nature cannot guide us in what we *should* do, we can learn quite a lot about what we *should not* do. There is, in other words, negative information available. It is a common assumption in ethics that one cannot be obliged to do what one is incapable of doing. (In fact no one has ever done what was impossible to do, even though some have done what they or others *thought* was impossible.) So one thing we can confidently say on the basis of this principle is that one ought not require someone to perform academically, or any other way, beyond the level they are capable of performing. Even then it is still not easy to avoid erring at times by overestimating ability and, perhaps more often and more seriously, underestimating ability. This is true of groups of children as well as of individuals. With respect to patterns of development of children as a group, it is important to know how according to nature they develop, so that teachers do not impose on them what they are incapable of accomplishing. To do so may lead to frustration and lasting damage to both student and teacher. That is why studies in child development and adolescent psychology, for example, are so important for teachers. But a caution is here in order. Often what is in fact a decision of value or a logical principle is passed off as a psychological law of nature. Maslow's hierarchy of needs, with basic needs for such things as food requiring satisfaction first and with the highest need for aesthetic experience coming last, is often thought of and asserted to be a pattern of human development necessitated by the nature of things instead of recognizing it for what it really is, a statement about how some people have been reared according to some people's values. Also sometimes logical principles are mistaken for psychological ones. The fact that children must learn basic elements of subtraction before learning how to do long division is a feature of the logic of arithmetic, not a feature of the natural development of children. In recent years Piaget's principles of children's cognitive development have been brought into question in a similar vein.

When the condition of universality for ascriptions of human nature is dropped, we can speak of individual natures of children. Children as individuals have, in addition to general patterns of development, individual apparently inborn tendencies and proclivities. Catering to such individual differences has long been thought to be important for teachers. Child-centered educators are particularly aware of such differences, but they are also likely to err by considering those differences to be more important than they really are. As with considerations about human nature for the class of children as a whole, consideration of individual differences pertains only to peripheral curricular matters. Individuals certainly do have different levels of ability and rates of learning, and it is useful to remind ourselves again that children cannot be required to do what they cannot do. But when it comes to key questions of content in curriculum, this will require decisions about the value of the content. Here observation of individual children is of little help. Even if it is observed that Susan is particularly interested and gifted in music, it does not follow that her curriculum be primarily music. If education is of such supreme value for everyone it is equally of value for Susan. Her individual capacity and ability certainly may play the crucial role in decisions regarding her career and specialized secondary studies, but not for her basic general education.

We have seen then that the central curriculum question, 'What shall we teach our children?' cannot, either for the 'traditional' or the 'progressive' educator be answered by appeal to 'needs', to 'human nature', nor to 'individual differences'. Ultimately decisions about the value of subject matter will have to be made. If it is education that we value supremely and seek to bring about, then we already have some rough guides as to the choice of subject-matter content. It will be that content that is functional in bringing about knowledge and understanding in breadth and depth within all the forms of rationality available to us. But even then, these are rough guides. Not everything of value can be taken up for careful study; there is just too much to know and too little time and resources. What then is the most valuable for all children to learn in a basic compulsory curriculum? Such questions will have to be answered by thoughtful citizens in every society but particularly by concerned parents and professionals. The role of the philosopher in this is to participate in the discussion and argument and to attempt to isolate the principles according to which the decisions can be made. So to conclude this chapter a few such principles are isolated to illustrate the kind of activity required.

Principles for Selecting Curriculum Content

What then are some principles according to which a curriculum specialist might select subject content for inclusion in a compulsory programme of study for purposes of general education?

1 Select that which cannot or is not likely to be understood or acquired without direct instruction or without directly engaging in it. (For a similar principle see John P. White (1973) *Towards a Compulsory Curriculum*, Routledge and Kegan Paul, Chapter 3.) The kinds of things that are envisaged are courses in pure mathematices, exact physical and

experimental sciences, appreciating the finest works of art, philosophy and second-order reflection. Corollaries of this principle are: (a) teach that which is difficult, not easy (algebra rather than mathematics for consumers); (b) teach the theoretical, not the practical (laws of physics rather than technology); (c) don't bother with what can be 'picked up' in any case (not cooking, pop music, trades). The reason for this principle is that to justify taking away someone's freedom (in this case, the student, by forcing him to come to school for study) we have to be very sure of the worthwhileness of so doing. The student must get something he could not without such compulsion achieve. What is the point of forcing a student away from his pastimes and his music to come to school only to be confronted with the same thing? That would hardly seem justified.

2   Select and teach that for which we have no alternative institutions in society. This is really a suggestion that the school's role be rather more limited, limited to a controlled, quiet, reflective place of study rather than a community centre offering many kinds of recreation and socialization facilities. Why, for example, should the school be involved in teaching how to play games?

3   Select that which contains generalizable truths and has wide-ranging application to life and illuminates many facets of life. Particularly select that which dwells on the enduring human thought, emotions, and concerns. Teach, for example, ethical principles, not the manners, vogues, and styles that conform to contemporary time; teach Shakespeare and Dostoevski, not comics and exclusively modern novels.

4   Select and teach that which leads to mastery of the structure and form of the logically distinct conceptual schemes represented by the various 'forms of knowledge' referred to in the last Chapter. This is what will develop in the student those qualities of mind which are the hallmark of the autonomous person. In sum, the curriculum should not cater to felt needs and interests of children and thus reflect what is in their nature. Rather it should challenge students to create for them new needs and give them interests they would otherwise not have dreamt of.

Suggested further readings:

DEARDEN, R.F. (1966) '"Needs" in education' in *British Journal of Educational Studies*, XIV, pp. 5–17.

HIRST, P.H. and PETERS, R.S. (1970) *op. cit.*, pp. 32–41.

LLOYD, D.I. (1976) 'Traditional and progressive education' in LLOYD, D.I. (Ed.) *Philosophy and the Teacher*, Routledge and Kegan Paul, pp. 89–100.

WILSON P.S. (1971) *Interest and Discipline in Education*, Routledge and Kegan Paul, chapters 1 and 2.

Notes

1 This has been done very effectively by LIOYD, D.I. (1976) 'Traditional and progressive education' in his edited book *Philosophy and the Teacher*, Routledge and Kegan Paul, pp. 89–100.

2 DEARDEN, R.F. (1966) '"Needs" in Education', in *British Journal of Educational Studies*, XIV, 3, p. x. Much of what follows is an adaptation of Dearden's ideas in this article.

3 OAKESHOTT, M. (1971) 'Education: The engagement and its frustration' in *British Journal of Educational Studies*, V, 1, p. 46.

4 Democritus, B33, Herman Diel's numbering.

Questions and Exercises

Answer the following:

1 Compare and contrast values espoused by 'traditionalists' and 'progressivists' in education.

2 Explain how an analysis of 'need' statements reveals that one cannot escape making value judgments in education by appeal to needs of children and students.

Answer the following questions as briefly as possible:

1 How are wants and interests of children related to what is good for children?

2 What is the problem of motivation in education? Can that problem be solved by appealing to children's needs? wants? interests? Explain.

3 What is the problem with attempting to base educational decisions on human nature?

Write a short essay on how you would go about planning a compulsory curriculum for the public school to ensure general education.

CHAPTER 7

Teaching and Learning and Education

In this chapter we will consider the processes of teaching and learning and what about them is educational. Sometimes teachers, particularly beginning teachers, think that as long as children are learning, educational objectives are being advanced and teaching is being properly conducted. But the learning that is occurring could be going on in the wrong manner or the content might be worthless, trivial, or even false. If so, education was not occurring. Furthermore it might be that the teacher was not teaching at all; supervision of learning is not teaching at all in some senses of the term. Or again the teacher might have been teaching but doing this in a wrong manner and thus frustrating educational ends. It is clear that not all teaching and learning is educational. So it is important to be clear about the concepts 'teaching' and 'learning' and other related notions such as 'indoctrination' to see how these are related to education.

The Concept 'Learning'

We will see very shortly that the concept 'teaching' is inexplicable without the concept 'learning'; so we will begin by taking a closer look at the concept 'learning'. Various analyses of the concept reveal that three criteria are considered central for the concept 'learning' in educational contexts, yielding a definition as follows: learning is intentionally coming to know (or believe, or perform, etc.) as a result of experience. The first criterion is *intentionality*. It highlights the demand that learning is an activity that one engages in with purpose and intention to come up to a certain standard. That some learning is of this sort few would doubt; that all learning is of this type would be objected to by those who believe in sleep learning,

learning by hypnosis, and learning through conditioning. Psychologists who study learning often define learning as any change in behavior not the result of maturation. It cannot be denied that certain behaviors are acquired through a process of conditioning where no intention occurs on the part of the person (or animal) acquiring the behavior; but in what sense one can call this 'learning' is the issue. Let us allow a 'loose' use of learning (L_1) in which *all* non-maturational changes in behavior are considered learning, including those resulting from unconscious 'experience' as in conditioning. In that sense Johnny mastering mathematics and his dog mastering some tricks are both said to be 'learning'. But there is a 'tighter' sense of learning (L_2) in which the dog is not learning because it is merely *re*acting instead of acting; and is said not to be learning because intentionality is absent and because there is no conscious experience.

That learning must be the result of *experience* is a second criterion for learning. It is because experience can be either conscious or unconscious that the two kinds of learning (L_1 and L_2 above) can be differentiated, although the notion of 'unconscious experience' is itself troublesome. Can something that happens to one of which one is not aware be called 'experience'? What *is* clear is that for educational purposes the experience must be of the conscious variety, and thus it is that L_2 is the use of 'learning' vital in discussions about education. The reason that experience is required at all as a condition of learning is that one can (or could, theoretically) have skills and abilities which one is born with and thus not need to acquire. It could not be said that one learnt these because they were not acquired as a result of experience. What is learnt must be build on a pre-existing structure based on experience. When that pre-existing experiential structure does not exist, the agent fails to learn because he is not 'ready' to learn. Learning 'readiness' is held by some to be a necessary condition of learning.[2] We will subsume this requirement under the 'experience' condition already noted.

Clearly a third condition for 'learning' is the one already alluded to several times: *mastery*. Learning always has an object (x), mastery of which is essential for learning to occur. This x could be a skill or an item of propositional knowledge or belief. The reason that 'or belief' is appended is that one can learn a belief which is not true; that is, one can learn lies and misrepresentations and so on. But even here there is required a certain kind of mastery, a certain coming up to standards. The standards are those that are required for considering a proposition to be entertained as true. In educational contexts the paradigm for mastery is coming to know true propositions.

Before leaving discussion on learning it should be noted that 'learning' can be used in both a task and an achievement sense. In the task sense 'learning' refers to the attempt to bring about mastery even though mastery is not yet fully achieved. An example would be Johnny in the process of learning the times table. Though he has been at it for a while and 'knows' something of them, he still makes errors and needs more practice. In the achievement sense of 'learn', Johnny has not learnt his times table, for here mastery is clearly a requirement. More often than not learning is used in the achievement sense. If without explanation it is said that Johnny learnt x, then it is assumed that Johnny has mastered x.

Also worth pointing out is that it is very difficult to answer the question, 'How does learning take place?' for the answer depends on what is learnt. There are as many forms of learning as there are kinds of learning objectives and the latter would appear to be almost endless. It is not therefore surprising that generalizable learning patterns and principles are few and far between and not easily established on a scientific basis. The variables, taking together both the variation in things to be learnt and various learning styles and conditions, are just too many.

The Concept 'Teaching'

'Teaching' as Polymorphous and Triadic

The concept 'teaching' is even more slippery and bendable than the concept 'learning'. Both terms, but particularly 'teaching', are said to be polymorphous, taking many forms. The terms accommodate a variety of users. It is possible, for example, to think of 'teaching' as falling into three broad areas of use.[3] One use is the *occupational* use and names what a person is typically engaged in as an occupation or a profession. Thus school administrators and counsellors are said to belong to the teaching profession, though they seldom teach. Even teachers who regularly teach are still teachers while on holiday. But they are then not teaching in the *enterprise* sense, that is, doing those things that teachers typically do when on the job, like distributing books and assignments, marking assignments, encouraging students to learn. But even these tasks are not the central *intellectual acts* of teaching which lie at the heart of teaching, namely, those acts of explanation, of illustration, of demonstrating, justifying, contrasting, and so on which treat the subject matter directly and make it available for learning by the student. Distinguishing these uses is only one way of approaching the teaching concept.

Other analysts have observed that 'teaching' can rightly be thought of in two senses: in the *achievement* sense and in the *task* sense. In the achievement sense, teaching implies learning. Those who insist that 'unless the student has learnt, the teacher has not taught' are using the term in the achievement sense. By analogy, those who insist that 'unless there was a buyer, the salesman did not sell' are using 'selling' in the achievement sense. The controversy over whether teaching implies learning can be settled in part by noting that there is a 'task' sense of teaching which is just as legitimate and perhaps used even more often. In the task sense teaching does not imply learning. An activity known as 'teaching' does not, according to this sense of 'teaching', result in successful learning. By analogy, the salesman can actually be involved in selling without there being a buyer for his product.

Still another preliminary observation about 'teaching' is that it is used, in the paradigm cases, in a triadic combination. We will call this the rule of triadicity, or the rule of double accusatives. That simply means that 'to teach' typically carries both a direct and an indirect object. A typical case is one in which T (a teacher) intentionally does something (describe, display, indicate, etc.) with X (the subject matter) with the intention that S (the student, the learner) learns X; that is, typically 'T teaches X to S'. The rule of triadicity thus rules out the possibility of making any literal sense of such slogans as: 'We teach children, not subjects' or its contrary. It is not possible to teach children without teaching them something and equally impossible to teach a subject to no one. Users of such slogans as the above clearly have something else in mind which needs clearer articulation. Perhaps what they have in mind is that in teaching there must be concern about the cognitive state of the pupil, which is an important point that will be more fully discussed as we now turn to an attempt to isolate the criteria for 'teaching'.

The Criteria for 'Teaching'

Acts of teaching are not specifiable in a general sort of way. It would be practically impossible to list all of the acts of teaching and then see what they had in common and thus deduce our criteria.

The reason for this is that almost any act could be taken as an act of teaching. Telling a story, showing a film, proving a point, drawing a picture, even standing on one's head and thousands of other acts can be teaching acts. It depends entirely on what is being taught and that depends on what one intends the learner to learn.[4] It was pointed out earlier in the section on 'The concept "Learning"' that the kinds of things that can be learnt are extremely vast and variable; and since in teaching one intends to bring about learning, it follows that the kinds of things that constitute teaching acts are as numerous as the kinds of things that can be learnt. It is for this reason that we noted earlier that the concept 'teaching' is explicable only in terms of 'learning', for the nature of the act of teaching depends on the intention one has regarding the learning that is to occur. Thus *intentionality* is central to the explication of the teaching concept. Even then, typical of the accommodating features of the concepts, there are some uses of 'to teach' which fall outside this criterion. We say, for example, that 'nature (or the environment) taught us', meaning that we learnt from nature, though nature had no intentions. Such usages must, however, be considered peripheral and metaphorical.

The second condition for 'teaching' is what we will call an act of *subject-matter display*. The teacher must do something with the subject-matter (illustrate it, demonstrate it, talk about it, etc.) to make his intention known to the learner. Hirst and Peters use the term 'indicating' to refer to this necessary act of teaching.[5] It is internal to the act of teaching and necessary to it, unlike the acts of complimenting, exhorting, or rewarding students, which are extrinsic to the teaching act. This distinction between activities internal and external to the act of teaching is reminiscent of Komisar's 'enterprise' and 'intellectual act' senses (see section on '"Teaching" as polymorphous and triadic').

A third condition for teaching is what we will call the *readiness* condition and refers to the learner's cognitive state. It can happen (and all too often does happen) that a teacher will display some subject-matter with the intention that someone learn it, and still not be teaching because it is in principle impossible for the student to learn it for the reason that the display is beyond the level of comprehension of the student. If a person expounded and elaborated upon theoretical physics to a normal three-year old, we would not say this was merely bad teaching but rather that it was not teaching at all. Not meeting the cognitive state of the student can also be a failure to teach for the reason that a student already knows the subject matter. What one already knows one cannot learn; and if one cannot learn something it cannot be displayed to that person in such a manner that he can reasonably be expected to learn it. Thus both over-teaching and under-teaching in their extreme forms verge off into non-teaching. In other words, teaching requires display of subject matter at the appropriate level. It points to the wisdom of the old adage that a good teacher places the subject within the grasp of the student but makes him stand on tip-toes to get it.

The above three conditions satisfy the task sense of 'teaching'. A possible definition then is: teaching is an act of appropriately displaying some subject matter with the intent that someone learn it. If one wished to go on to provide the sufficient conditions for the achievement sense of 'teaching', it would still be too strong a demand that successful learning be the outcome. That would make the logical connection between learning and teaching too tight. A suggestion to avoid this problem is to make mastery attempts on the part of the learner a sufficient condition in the 'achievement' sense of teaching. Thus one can say that one had been successful in teaching when the learner made the attempt to learn. In most cases those attempts will also result in successful learning; but it is not necessary.

Relationships Between Education, Teaching, and Learning

Earlier in the book a fairly thorough study of the concept of education was undertaken. Having now also, though more briefly, examined the concepts of learning and teaching, we are in a position to trace some connections between these three. We shall comment on the relationship in each case after tracing the logical connections in a formal way, using the following symbols: L = learning; T = teaching; E = education; (t) = task; (a) = achievement; $\supset$ = imply; $\not\supset$ = does not imply; and $(\cdot)$ = 'and'.

Logical Connections[6]

The logical connection *between learning and teaching* is summed up in the following four propositions:

(a) $L_{(t)}$ or $L_{(a)}$ $\not\supset$ $T_{(t)}$ or $T_{(a)}$

Neither the task nor the achievement senses of learning imply teaching in any sense. This is because learning *can* (logically) take place without teaching. The connection is contingent only, which means that there may well be an empirical connection, depending on the facts in the case; but the connection is not logically necessary. We will comment on this contingent connection below.

(b) $T_{(t)} \not\supset L_{(t)}$ or $L_{(a)}$

The task sense of teaching implies neither the task nor the achievement sense of learning.

(c) $T_{(a)} \not\supset L_{(a)}$

The achievement sense of teaching does not imply the achievement sense of learning.

(d) $T_{(a)} \supset L_{(t)}$

The achievement sense of teaching implies the task sense of learning. We noted above that this suggestion was made to account for those uses of 'to teach' that intuitively demand consideration of teaching success.

The logical connection *between learning and education* is summed up in the following two propositions:

(a) $E \supset L_2$ (not L_1)

Education implies learning. Without learning there can be no education. Furthermore, the learning required is of the kind in which the achievement of certain standards is the result of conscious experience. This is because both the knowledge condition and the procedural condition for education require understanding; and understanding cannot come about through processes such as conditioning. The procedural condition requires that the voluntariness of the learner not be violated, as could be the case if L_1 learning (i.e., conditioning) were allowed.

(b) L_1 or $L_2 \not\supset E$

In neither the loose nor tight sense of learning does learning imply education. This is because of the value criterion built into the concept education. As noted in the introduction to this unit, learning could be trivial, worthless, or even false. It follows that merely a healthy learning environment does not at all guarantee education.

The logical connection between *teaching and education* is summed up in the following proposition:

$$T_{(t)} \text{ or } T_{(a)} \not\supset E \cdot E \not\supset T_{(t)} \text{ or } T_{(a)}$$

Teaching in any sense does not imply education and education does not imply teaching in any sense. Even if teaching implied learning, there would be no logical connection, since learning itself does not imply education. But teaching does not even imply learning, so the logical distance between teaching and education is even greater.

However, to say that there is no logical connection between teaching and education is of course not to say there is not an important empirical or contingent connection. To trace this contingent connection is also to provide an answer to why we should teach at all.

Contingent Connections

If teaching is not logically necessary for learning and as a result, not for education, why then do we teach? Since this is not primarily a philosophical question, only a general and partial answer to the question will be entertained here.

One reason for teaching, so the well-warranted assumption goes, is that most things are more rapidly and reliably learnt when teaching does go on. Not everyone would agree with this assumption. Those who are keen advocates of 'learning by discovery', for example, would argue that it is precisely because 'discovery', methods lead to more effective learning that teaching should be abandoned in favour of 'facilitation of learning'. In Komisar's terms teachers would engage in the 'enterprise' but not the 'intellectual act' sense of teaching. It is of course a moot point at what stage 'discovery' methods verge over from teaching into mere supervision of learning. But given that the distinction can be made it is still a questionable matter whether everything that is worth learning for eductional purposes needs to be taught in the tight sense of the term outlined in the section on 'The concept "teaching"'. A reasonable case could be made that some teachers teach too much. Others, of course, teach far too little. When to teach and when not to teach in a formal learning setting such as the school is a debatable question and one for a professional teacher's judgment. What is much less debatable is the continued need for schools with teachers to ensure that educationally valuable learning continues even if the judgment is not to teach directly; and this takes us to the second main reason why we teach. The teacher's judgment is required to ensure that the content to be learnt has educational merit. The teacher helps to ensure that worthwhile knowledge is included in the curriculum and the not worthwhile is excluded. The teacher helps to ensure a well-rounded education. Yet another reason for teaching is that the abstract nature and complex structure of educational objectives are difficult to reach without the help of a teacher. The laws of physics, the theorems of geometry, the principles of ethics, the theories of history, and the criteria for assessing good art are very hard to come by without these being in some sense taught.

Another reason teaching is essential is to ensure that students develop attitudes of open-mindedness, criticism, tolerance, and humility as well as other rational capacities characteristic of the educated person. The educated teacher helps to prevent forms of miseducation, chief of which is indoctrination. Since indoctrination is fundamentally at odds with education, since it is still often damagingly practised in schools, and since it is often confused with other forms of miseducation, an analysis of the concept and a discussion of its distinguishing features will be undertaken to conclude this chapter.

Indoctrination and Other Forms of Miseducation

Some Forms of Miseducation

Practices related to teaching which are deleterious to education are numerous. Over-teaching; under-teaching; no teaching when teaching is called for; imbalanced teaching (one subject to the exclusion of others) resulting in lack of breadth and roundedness in education; undermining educational objectives of the school by usurping school authority for political or social purposes; gearing schooling to technical training — these are all forms of miseducation but none need involve indoctrination. Indoctrination also is not necessarily involved in giving false information; in transmitting undesirable attitudes such as cynicism, disrespect, slovenliness; giving false impressions (details do not matter; education is easy); using propaganda; commanding children; drilling in content; compelling children; threatening and rewarding children; or punishing children. Some of these practices may at times be necessary and legitimate; most likely they are deleterious to education. But they are not to be confused with indoctrination. The point to be emphasized is that there are numerous ways a teacher may err which have nothing to do with indoctrination. Exactly which types of error fall within the practice of indoctrination is a matter of some dispute. Philosophers just seem not to agree on what indoctrination is. Just what the problem is with indoctrination will depend to some extent on what one concludes are the main conditions for the use of the term.

The Concept 'Indoctrination'

While controversy over the meaning of 'indoctrination' continues, it is fairly widely accepted that indoctrination is (1) pejorative and (2) related to beliefs. Historically, it was not always the case that indoctrination was thought of as something negative. But in recent times accusations of indoctrination raise eye-brows; and indoctrination is something one definitely does not want one's children to undergo. Few disagree. Also generally accepted is that indoctrination is broadly concerned with beliefs rather than with conditioned response. Even then some people mistakenly and carelessly say they have been 'indoctrinated to be afraid of policemen'. Such error is understandable since attitudes sometimes are a combination of belief and conditioned response. But where beliefs of any kind are absent, such as automatic aversion to crowds, there cannot be any thought of indoctrination; only conditioned response. But agreement on the negative quality of indoctrination and on the fact that indoctrination is concerned with beliefs still leaves the central issue of the meaning of indoctrination undecided. We still want to know exactly what we as teachers should not do if we are to avoid indoctrination. A number of views have been suggested by philosophers centering around four criterial attributes of indoctrination, which will now be considered.

Method

Some people take the view that the distinguishing feature of indoctrination is the method it uses for presenting material. Indoctrination for them is a particularly bad way of *how* teaching is done. They cite as examples such practices as rote learning, recitaton, lack of discussion, and presenting only one side of controversial issues. But when they are asked to provide an exhaustive list of the methods indoctrinators use, they are hard pressed; for they would have to admit that indoctrinators at times use methods that are not very different from regular good teaching. Indoctrinators do sometimes explain and allow questioning. The fact that they might not explain adequately and do allow only questions that further their cause is not a deficiency in the *method* they use but a deficiency of another kind. In fact the methods indoctrinators use could be divided into three kinds: (1) those that are legitimate regular classroom teaching practices such as memorization, recitation, drill, telling, explaining, modelling, illustrating, instancing, repetition, monitoring, rote learning, and so on; (2) those that are frowned upon as poor or unimaginative teaching but are also used by indoctrinators, such as no discussion, peer group appeal, failure to explain adequately, cynicism and brow-beating, use of rhetoric, threatening, use of charisma and charm, use of coercion and punishment, use of social sanction, and so on; (3) those of a more nefarious kind that are typically, but not exclusively, used by indoctrinators, such as selective use of evidence, over-generalization from insufficient instances, use of authority as 'stoppers' to discussion; toleration of inconsistency, contradiction, and circularity of argument; suppression of counter-evidence; distortion of evidence; use of programmatic definitions; failure to suggest available alternative points of view; lying; disregard for criticism; use of selected criticism; misrepresentation of the status of beliefs; isolation from contrary influence; use of 'loaded' questions, and so on. The reason that methods in this latter group are used is that the nature of the content of indoctrination demand it. The reason that inadequate explanation is used as a method, for example, is that the content is not adequately explain-*able*. Such methods are regarded as indoctrination because of the nature of the content transmitted. Indoctrinatory method depends on indoctrinatory content. Is there then, in other words, no general principle according to which a method of teaching can be classified as being or not being indoctrinatory apart from content? That is what will be argued below. But before we turn to that we want to consider whether that criterion might not be the aims or intentions of the indoctrinator.

Aims or Intentions
Those who hold to the 'intention' criterion, like M. Degenhardt[7], propose that 'to indoctrinate is to do anything with the intention of getting people to hold views in a fixed, unquestioning way'. Whether the views are true or false does not matter; nor does use of a particular method matter. What is crucial is the aim or intention of the teacher. Presumably, on this view, if a teacher intended a student to hold a firm view 'once and for all', say, on the spelling of the word 'chrysanthemum' or on the date Caesar crossed the Rubicon, then, no matter if the teacher used as much explanation as the content would allow and further used drill and review to fix the content in the student's mind, the teacher could rightfully be ac-

cused of indoctrination. Degenhardt[8] says that such a use of indoctrination would (1) accord with current usage and (2) pinpoint what it is about indoctrination that is negative. On both accounts, it would appear, he is wrong. If in the above examples, and any other examples of fixing ideas firmly in students' minds, we are accused of indoctrination, then every teacher who teaches spelling, reading, arithmetic, indeed almost any subject, can be accused of indoctrination. We just do not so accuse them. Nor do we think that such teaching is negative. Indeed we assess success in such teaching to the degree that these elementary things are fixed in students' minds. If, however, a teacher intends *and succeeds* in fixing in children's minds the idea that if they are not good God will punish them, then one can properly call that indoctrination. That does accord with current usage and pinpoints what is negative about indoctrination. But note, the reason for properly calling this indoctrination is the *content* of what is fixed, not the mere fact that something is fixed. Note too, that the proper use of indoctrination for this case depends on the intention having effect in fact. Intention is insufficient for calling some activity indoctrination. Not only is there the difficulty of not knowing what someone's intentions are apart from the methods used and the content taught, but there is also the problem of not being able to accommodate unintentional indoctrination or failing in the intention to indoctrinate, both of which do occur, and which Degenhardt to his credit does realize.

To shift the criterion from 'intention' to success or 'results' does not significantly improve matters.

Results or manner

The view that 'results' constitute the definitive attribute of indoctrination highlights the point that to be indoctrinated is in fact to hold views in a fixed, unquestioning way. Reference is to the manner in which one holds beliefs rather than to the content of the belief or the intention of the teacher or the method the teacher used. This view of indoctrination does avoid the problems of unintended indoctrination or failed intentions to indoctrinate. But it still does not pinpont what is negative about indoctrination nor does it accord with standard usage. The points made above in the section on 'Aims or intentions' regarding the importance of the content of the beliefs is still crucial. And the 'results' view invites other problems, which Degenhardt also has singled out. He notes that:

> (I)t doesn't seem quite right to settle for defining indoctrination exclusively in terms of the way in which someone ends

up holding a particular belief ... (for it is) odd to talk of indoctrination where someone holds rigidly fixed beliefs, not because of anything that has been done to him, but because he is too stupid or too idle to think things out for himself.[9]

Degenhardt then argues that indoctrination is something done to someone by another or others. This is probably usually true in fact, but is not a necessary condition. For could someone not on his own deliberately come to hold in a fixed, unquestioning manner a set of beliefs which are doctrinaire? Could he not indoctrinate himself? And would this not depend on the nature of the beliefs he has come to hold in this unquestioning manner? Holding beliefs unquestioningly is not always and inherently negative or irrational. Most of us have never questioned the spelling of certain words, the verity of $1 + 1 = 2$, or the law of the non-contradiction. And most of us do not even know how to question those things. What is inherently negative and irrational and is picked up by the term 'indoctrinated' is failure to question certain types of questionable beliefs. It is of course not easy to know which beliefs are questionable and which are not. Perhaps most beliefs are potentially questionable. That is why an open mind and a critical attitude are generally accepted values in education. But not every anti-educational value or activity is indoctrination, although indoctrination is essentially anti-educational. It is anti-educational precisely because it closes the mind where it should be open; it encourages acceptance where criticism is necessary; it fails to question a particular kind of belief. And so we come finally to consider content of belief as the distinguishing attribute of indoctrination.

Content

In arguing for 'content' as the central criterion for indoctrination, no attempt will here be made to summarize all the arguments that can and have been given. Since these arguments are readily available for an interested reader, only a few of the arguments will be summarized and a few additional ones presented.

The core idea behind the content argument is that a particular kind of belief, namely doctrine, is the key to understanding what indoctrination is. The argument is *not* that because 'indoctrination' is etymologically related to 'doctrine' that the connection between the two exists. It is rather that because there is the connection that the words are etymologically related. Nor is the argument that since controversial ideas and doctrines are synonymous, and since indoctrination is connected to doctrines, that therefore indoctrination is the passing on of controversial ideas. That argument errs in equating controversial ideas with doctrines. Doctrines certainly are controversial; but not all controversial ideas are doctrines. Controversy can rage over whether or not the wave or particle theory of light accounts for more of the facts; but neither theory is doctrine. Doctrine is a particular type of controversial idea, which will be described shortly. Failure to recognize various types of controversial beliefs leads some theorists to reject without warrant the content arguments.

Degenhardt, for example, construes the 'content' theorists as dividing all areas of thought into either well founded objective knowledge such as mathematics and science on the one hand and areas of mere belief such as politics, religion, and morals on the other hand. He goes on to construe them as saying that the former are not controversial and thus not subject to indoctrination while the latter are controversial and so subject to indoctrination. This view Degenhardt finds oversimplified and thus he dismisses the 'content' theorists. The view is over-simplified, but it is not the view espoused by anyone associated with the theory defended here. Yes, scientific theories are controversial, but they are nevertheless not subject to indoctrination because they are not doctrines. Yes, certain political and moral principles are not controversial and can be taught without fear of indoctrination. The objections Degenhardt raises just are not objections to content theorists. And in the one objection he does make against them he begs the question.[10] He argues against the 'content' view because that would mean that the teaching of politics and religion would count as indoctrination and hence be disapproved of. So because Degenhardt wants to make room for the teaching of politics and religion he misconstrues the content theorists and rejects the 'content' view. But this answers in advance his question about the meaning of indoctrination. He fails to notice that it is a particular type of controversial belief, namely doctrine, which is the source of objection in the teaching of politics and religion. What then is doctrine?

Following the lead of A.C. Kazepides[11] we shall consider the following as characteristics of doctrines:

1 Doctrines are beliefs. This, as already noted, will differentiate doctrines from attitudes and conditioned responses and from socialized reactions.
2 Doctrinal beliefs are non-verifiable. This means that they are more problematic than beliefs which are just not so far

been proven true or false. They are in principle incapable of being proved true; they are unverif*iable*, not merely unverified. This further means that they are also not falsifiable. A proposition that could not be false also could not be true. The fundamental problem with doctrines is that there are no conceivable ways of determining their truth or falsity. Examples of such doctrines are: 'The pope is infallible'; 'God loves us all'; 'The rise of the working class and the withering away of the state are inevitable'; 'All historical events are causally determined by prior historical events'.

3　Doctrines are pronouncements of charismatic leaders or authorities as part of a wider system of beliefs. They are planks in ideologies and as such are of momentous concern to those who propagate and believe them.

4　Doctrines are statements of belief that are ultimately related to practice. That is why they are beliefs around which whole ways of life are determined.

5　Doctrines are held to be self-evident.

6　Doctrines are essentially controversial because the grounds for believing in them is absent.

It is because politics and religion are replete with doctrines that they are usually not taught as such in state-supported public schools in liberal democracies, although there is considerable teaching *about* politics and religion. The distinction between religious and political education and education about religion and politics is important to keep in mind in connection with indoctrination. The former is essentially indoctrinatory; the latter can be accomplished in an open-minded, critically thoughtful manner, characteristic of the educated person.

Suggested further readings:

CHAMBERS, J.H. (1983) *The Achievement of Education*, New York, Harper and Row, pp. 34–47.

DEGENHARDT, M.A.B. (1976) 'Indoctrination' in LLOYD, D.I. (Ed.), *Philosophy and the Teacher*, London, Routledge and Kegan Paul, pp. 19–29.

KAZEPIDES, A.C. (1973) 'The grammar of indoctrination' in *Philosophy of Education 1973*: Proceedings of the Philosophy of Education Society, Illinois.

SNOOK, I. (1972) *Concepts of Indoctrination*, London, Routledge and Kegan Paul.

Notes

1 See, for example, HIRST, P.H. and PETERS, R.S. (1970) *The Logic of Education*, London, Routledge and Kegan Paul. pp. 74–76.
2 See FLEMING, K.G. (1976) *The Epistemological Character of the Relation between the Concepts of Teaching and Learning*, PhD Thesis, University of London.
3 See KOMISAR, B.P. (1968) in 'Teaching: Act and enterprise' in J. MACMILLAN, C.B.J. and NELSON, T.W. (Eds.), *Concepts of Teaching*, Chicago, Rand McNally.
4 See in this connection HIRST, P.H. (1974) 'What is teaching?' in *Knowledge and the Curriculum*, London, Routledge and Kegan Paul, pp.101-115.
5 See HIRST, P.H. and PETERS, R.S. (1970) *op. cit.*, p. 79.
6 For a fuller discussion of the logical relationships between teaching, learning, and education see K.G. Fleming, 'Criteria of learning and teaching', *Jounral of Philosophy of Education*, 14, 1, 1980, pp. 39–51. Most of what is included in this section is based on that work including some of the phrasing.
7 In LLOYD, D.I. (Ed.) (1976) *Philosophy and the Teacher*, London, Routledge and Kegan Paul, Chapter 2.
8 *Ibid.*, p. 23.
9 *Ibid.*, p. 26.
10 *Ibid.*, p. 23.
11 See his 'The grammar of indoctrination' in *Philosophy of Education 1973*: Proceedings of the Philosophy of Education Society, 1973. Also see his 'Indoctrination, doctrines, and the foundations of rationality' in the same journal, 1987.

Questions and Exercises

Answer the following questions in a paragraph or two:
1 What necessary conditions must be met before one can describe an activity as a teaching activity?
2 Trace the *logical* connections between teaching, learning, and education.
3 Is teaching success dependent on student learning?
4 Is 'learning' an achievement term?
5 What are doctrines?
6 How are doctrines and indoctrination related?

Answer the following questions in a few sentences each:
1 In which areas of study is the charge of indoctrination most likely to arise?
2 Is it necessary to indoctrinate very young children before they reach the age of reason?
3 The term 'teaching' is typically used with double accusatives. Explain.

4 Is it in principle possible to provide an exhaustive list of teaching activities? Why or Why not?
5 Is it possible to indoctrinate people with rationality?

Make a list of all the methods (or techniques) of teaching you can think of which might be considered methods of indoctrination. Now look at your list again and ask yourself whether some (or all) of these methods might not at some time or other be used in teaching (including the not so good teaching) without your being accused of indoctrination. What does this exercise tell you about the nature of indoctrination?

Decide whether the following sentences are true or false. Then for each, write a one sentence explanation of why you think so.
1 Unless the student has learnt, the teacher hasn't taught.
2 Unless the child learns by discovery he is being indoctrinated.
3 You can teach yourself all you need to learn about riding bicycles.
4 Non-teaching school administrators are still teachers.
5 You can learn without getting it right.
6 Learning is all non-maturational change in behaviour.
7 There are some good kinds of indoctrination.
8 Nature taught him to survive in the woods.

Write a short essay on one of the following questions:
1 Is religious education without indoctrination possible?
2 Is moral education without indoctrination possible?
3 Is political education without indoctrination possible?

CHAPTER 8

Inter-personal and Social Issues in Education

In the last chapter we argued that education for everyone can best be accomplished through systematic teaching in schools. Such a system, if for no other reason than the sheer numbers of children involved and the compulsory nature of attendance, will inevitably require some sort of structure and organization. As a consequence issues concerning discipline, punishment, freedom and authority, and the appropriate student-teacher relationship arise. These issues are to a large extent sociological and psychological, requiring specific empirical information for resolution, and so fall outside the domain of philosophy. There are, however, philosophical dimensions to these issues which will be addressed here. One of the problems concerns the meaning of terms such as 'discipline' and 'authority'; another problem concerns the justification for the use of such measures as punishment. These sorts of questions will be our primary concern in this chapter.

Discipline

The notion of 'discipline' is a case in point. Discipline is often confused with punishment. Yet those who reject punishment as a legitimate measure of control over children are reluctant to dismiss discipline. For them there is obviously a connection between discipline and punishment but the connection is not clear. It is therefore important to sort this out and to try to pinpoint the importance of discipline in education and to relegate punishment to its proper place.

The Concept 'Discipline'

The central notion of discipline is that of submission to rules. These rules are usually the structure of what has to be learnt. Hence one can explain the origin of 'discipline' from the Latin 'disco' which means 'I learn'. Hence also one can explain the term 'discipline' when reference is made to a subject of study, such as the discipline of biology.

The kinds of rules to which one must submit in order to be disciplined are various. First, there are rules which are related to the subject matter itself, such as rules of grammar, rules for properly conducting scientific experiments, and rules of mathematical reasoning, and so on. There are, secondly, rules related to the manner of learning something, such as rules about concentration, about practice and review, about note-taking, and so on. Thirdly, certain rules obtain for the efficient operation of schools, such as rules about attendance, movement through the school, emergency measures, and so on. There are also rules overlapping with those just mentioned that are of a moral nature and apply outside of school as well as inside. Such rules as taking turns, telling the truth, refraining from bullying and injury, and so on are not merely operational conveniences in the running of a school but more generally part of one's moral education. In any one of the above ways one can be disciplined. And if one is to obtain an education it is easy to see that one must necessarily become disciplined. Education without discipline is impossible. That is not true of punishment. As we shall see below, punishment may at times be helpful in establishing discipline, but it is not a necessary logical condition for education nor a necessary empirical condition for education, as is discipline.

Forms of Discipline

Discipline can be self-imposed, externally imposed, or be imposed in a manner combining these two. It is self-imposed if an individual accepts and complies with the rules on his own without external pressure. A self-disciplined person is one who imposes on himself conformity to rules either because he delights in and sees merit in the rules themselves, as when someone seeks out the conditions under which plants grow because it is inherently interesting, or because doing so is a means to something else one wants, as when someone seeks conditions for plant growth because he needs food.

Self-discipline is most desirable in education because:

1 it encourages autonomy in the individual, thought to be desirable as an educational goal;
2 it is more efficient in the achievement of learning; and
3 it develops and reflects those valuable states of mind characteristic of the educated person.

Discipline is externally imposed when someone else — a teacher or parent, most likely – manipulates an individual to submit to rules not of his own choosing by playing on his fears and desires. Rewards and sanctions are presented as motivation for learning. In this way there is created an artificial connection between what is wanted and discipline. Hirst and Peters say of externally imposed discipline:

> So in learning what has to be learnt the child is learning an irrelevant connection as well as developing an instrumental attitude. In the cases of self-imposed discipline, on the other hand, the connection between the submission to rules and what is wanted is not so artificial.[1]

Because of this artificiality, because of the extra effort and attention required by the teacher, because of the lack of autonomy on the part of the learner, and because manipulation of others is, other things equal, inherently ethically repulsive, it seems reasonable on the face of it to avoid imposing discipline externally. The difficulty, however, is that other things are not equal. Children frequently just are not motivated sufficiently to impose on themselves the discipline necessary for obtaining a well-rounded education. It is a common phenomenon that children's wants and interests and the corresponding readiness to impose self-discipline are developed by a process of originally imposing discipline on them externally until, and by means of which, self-discipline is realized. There is in this development a stage at which discipline in neither completely externally imposed nor self-imposed. It is somewhat of an intermediate type.

Discipline of a hybrid type is an extremely important process in education and is best illustrated by the child or student modelling himself after the teacher. Here the child is not being imposed upon directly; he does want to behave or perform in a manner which is demonstrated by the model. To some extent the child is imposing on himself the rules of behavior and of performance he sees represented. At the same time the teacher is deliberately confronting the child with model performance and activity, including such educationally worthwhile activities as carefully arguing a point, neatly and efficiently deriving a mathematical proof, or demonstrating precise, clear, and readable prose. This form of modelling may in fact be the paradigm for a gradual shift from external to self-imposed discipline.

Sometimes it is paramount that children submit to rules, particularly rules of practice and rules of behavior injurious to others, even though they are unwilling to discipline themselves to do so. In such cases measures such as punishment can be taken to enforce discipline.

Punishment

Punishment is a notion fairly easily grasped. Most of the issues concerning punishment relate to its use and justifiability in education and educational settings; and most of this section will be related to those issues. But to begin with we shall draw the distinction between discipline and punishment more sharply by focussing on the concept punishment.

The Concept 'Punishment'

Punishment is fairly completely defined as: the intentional infliction of pain or unpleasantness by an authority on an offender for a breach of a social rule. It will be noted that the definition contains five necessary elements. First, the act of punishment cannot be a fortuitous event or happening. It cannot be done accidentally. If a bully accidentally falls and hurts himself, that will not count as punishment, however painful it is, because it was not done intentionally by an authority. Secondly, punishment must be painful or unpleasant. Often teachers mistakenly think they are 'punishing' children by making them stay after hours when the children enjoy the attention and being in the company of the teacher. No wonder the teacher complains that 'punishing' children does not work. Failure to punish in these cases is failure to inflict pain or unpleasantness. Reform, of course, can be brought about without infliction of pain; but only if infliction of pain is present can one talk of punishment as a method of reform. Thirdly, punishment must be enacted by someone whose authority to do so has been established. A victim of bullying who strikes back is not punishing the bully precisely because he is not in a position of authority to do so. Such retaliation is merely a form of revenge. Fourthly, the infliction of pain or unpleasantness must be on an offender. It might be possible to achieve the desired results of punishment, such as deterrence, by inflicting pain on someone other than the offender, perhaps on a relative of the offender or someone the offender likes. This would not count as punishment because there is written into the concept of punishment the notion of fairness; and this means, further, that for logical reasons the innocent cannot be punished. The teacher who deprives a whole class of privileges because a single undetected person has committed an offence should keep that in mind. Whatever else the treatment of the whole class is, it is not punishment. Finally, punishment entails infliction of pain on an offender for a breach of a social rule. This condition is actually an elaboration of the fourth condition, since the notion of 'offender' already entails the kind of culpability which deliberate breaching of rules results in.

It is worth emphasizing that in punishment the rule for which one is punished is a rule of behavior, not a rule internal to subject matter. One is not punished for an error in arithmetic, say, unless the error is made deliberately, in which case it is not merely an arithmetical mistake. One cannot be guilty of inability to understand. Nevertheless, one can be guilty of not applying oneself. So it is not quite right to say that one is guilty, and therefore punishable, *only* on the condition that a social or behavior rule be broken *deliberately*; for one can still be guilty of a breach of rule as a result of neglect or ignorance. The guilt arises from breaching rules against neglect and ignorance. One could interpret this as deliberately indulging oneself and for that reason become guilty of neglect and ignorance; but that still is not to say that a particular rule was breached deliberately. The point to emphasize is that people place themselves into the class of the punishable because of their responsibility for action. The concept 'punishment' does not make sense in a deterministic conception of human behavior. Where all behavior is said to be 'caused' by events and forces impinging on the agent, and the action of the agent then interpreted as the response or reaction to those forces, there can only be 'negative reinforcement' to eliminate certain responses, but no punishment. In such a world there are no outlaws; there are only disturbed cowboys. Or, as in *West Side Story*, there are no depraved; only the deprived. There are, of course, situations where children in schools are deprived, disturbed, or socially and psychologically sick. These children should not (cannot, logically) be punished; morality requires that only the guilty but not the sick be punished. But it is quite wrong to think of all misbehaviors as being of the deterministic kind. Some children do deliberately break social rules and place themselves within the group of the punishable.

Having determined that people are punishable is not, however, the same as having provided adequate grounds for the use of punishment. The latter depends on whether or not one can provide a sound justification for the use of it.

The Justification for the Use of Punishment

The justification for the use of punishment in general is discussed in the literature under three broadly conceived reasons for punishing:

1　retribution;
2　deterrence and prevention; and
3　reform.

We shall consider these in turn and see whether the reasons apply in educational situations.

Retribution

The notion of retribution is summed up in the maxim: an eye for an eye and a tooth for a tooth. It is essentially the idea of getting even or settling a score. The source of this idea often is in a religious position, or simply an intuition, or seen as obvious in nature. It rests on the view that it just is wrong that some people should break rules of a moral nature and get away with it. The attractiveness of the idea is its appeal to some sense of fairness. Unquestionably, as already noted, there is in the idea of punishment a notion of fairness. But whether this constitutes a justification for using punishment is another matter. One does not do something or other because of what a word means; to do so is yet once again an attempt to commit the naturalistic fallacy.[2] In *Ethics and Education*, Peters says that

> 'Punishment' *must* involve 'retribution'; for 'retribution' implies doing something to someone in return for what he has done.... Punishment is one type of retributive transaction.... (It) must be retributive — by definition.... But definitions settle no substantial questions.... It is one thing to understand what is meant by 'punishment'; it is quite another to give good reasons why punishment should exist (pp. 268–269).

There is then no law of nature that says punishment must exist; nor can we find justification in the meaning of punishment. And intuition is not itself a justification; intuitions themselves need to be justified. So there is in the concept of retribution no justification for punishment in general. And so retribution is also no justification for the use of punishment in schools.

Deterrence and Prevention

These two notions usually are mentioned together since they can apply to the same person; but essentially they are different. The deterrent effect of the social institution of punishment is on those who in the wider community observe offenders punished. Because they see what happens to offenders, they themselves are discouraged from committing similar offences. The prevention notion can apply to those same people, but more often refers to those who have once offended and been punished for it and as a result are prevented from repeat offences. It is a prevention of recidivism. These two notions together have the effect of maintaining order in a society by the upholding of rules or laws; and that is one justification for the use of punishment.

The assumption is that punishment does in fact have the effect of deterrence and prevention. Some people claim that punishment does not have that effect and, because it breeds negativism, should not be used. True; sometimes punishment does not have the deterrent or preventative effect; and if it never or seldom did, one could not use deterrence as an argument. But it can fairly confidently be said that often, perhaps usually, it does work. These matters of fact can be settled only by careful empirical investigation; and one must not be too hasty to assert adamantly without evidence. But we shall here continue to assume that it does work, both for reasons of surface evidence and for commonsense reasons in human motivation, namely, that people do by and large attempt to avoid painful or unpleasant situations.

So let us assume that punishment works in the manner required. Does it follow that if punishment works, it should therefore be used? No, it certainly does not. If, as noted earlier, the overall purpose is to uphold rules and laws in a social group, are there not ways in which this can be done that are more humane than, and preferable to, the use of punishment? This line of reasoning is certainly correct. For moral reasons, pain is inherently bad. So measures taken to avoid it are always preferable to those which needlessly incur it. This means that if reason and persuasion, or even pleasurable reward, can be used to get people to uphold reasonable rules of conduct they are to be preferred to the use of punishment. Punishment is therefore a measure of last resort. Only when other measures fail is the infliction of pain through the use of punishment justified. But it is in the end justified because the negative results of not using it are greater than the pain induced. It is the utilitarian maxim of temporary pain for long term gain.

The above general argument for the justification of punishment applies in the classroom as well. The 'last resort' argument is even stronger in the case of children in school. In the case of adults it can fairly be assumed that they know the rules and reasons for them. Arguments given them are often a waste of time, for they know them all. In the case of children, learning the rules is one of the reasons for their being in school. They still do not fully understand the rules or the reasons for them. Too, their memories are very short; and often simple reminders will do in place of punishment. Punishment, if overused, also creates a negative attitude to the teacher and to learning in schools generally. For these, as well as for the moral considerations already noted, punishment should be used only as a last resort. But as a last resort it is justified for reasons of deterrence and prevention.

To be effective in deterring others, punishment should be predictable, fairly and fittingly enacted, and made public. Those who punish children secretly to protect the child's ego are losing an important effect of punishment. Also if the child being punished is ego-deficient enough for it to be a factor, it is doubtful that the child should be punished at all. But given that children are not socially or psychologically disturbed (and, granted, it is often difficult to decide on borderline cases) they should be treated similarly for similar breaches of rules. This is simply applying the moral consideration of fairness. The rules, too, must be well known, for culpability is not easily established when rules are vague and poorly promulgated. What kind of punishment is fitting is a matter of some controversy. Apart from noting that the severity of the punishment must fit the severity of the breach of rules (and presumably children learn something about the range of importance of the various rules this way), there is very little that is agreed upon with respect to fittingness. Why thieves should be jailed, speeders fined, talkers kept in after school, or bullies made to clean up the school yard seems to be either pure convention or complete arbitrariness. In recent years, notions such as 'punishment must fit the crime' have been rethought and attempts made to give 'fittingness' a new twist under the guise of 'children learning from the consequences of their action'. Since such views seem to reject punishment altogether and since they are finding a significant place in pedagogical thinking generally, we shall delay discussion of this for later. The focus of such learning seems to be reform, rather than deterrence and prevention. Reform is indeed another very important consideration in the justification for the use of punishment.

Reform

Reform, the notion of making people better by bringing them back from lapsed states, is another reason used to justify applying punishment on offenders. The problem with this type of justification is that there is only skimpy evidence that in general it works. The idea that people in general will obey a rule to avoid pain seems ever so much more acceptable than the idea that a person, *because* he is punished, actually comes to understand the reasonableness of a rule and thus becomes better by adopting that rule as his own and abiding by it. The question of how punishment, rather than thought and explanation, in general can provide insight is puzzling enough. Perhaps all punishment can do is shock one into thinking or alert one to an explanation. So in a roundabout way punishment could lead to reform in adults. But, in children, who have not yet been 'formed', it is difficult to see how punishment could reform them. To *some* extent this could be possible, depending on the age and sophistication of the child; most children are after all en route to becoming adults and have some adult characteristics, including formed ideas, rules, and attitudes from which they can slip. But in the main, it is not likely that reform can be a major consideration for using punishment on children.

It seems quite clear, then, that the major justification for the use of punishment is upholding of rules of behaviour in schools by way of deterrence and prevention. Punishment as a device for bringing about learning of the subject matter is not likely to be of much avail, neither for academic subjects in general nor for reform and moral learning in particular. In fact, because of the negativism connected with punishment, some people have argued that punishment can be rejected altogether in favour of getting children to learn from the consequences of their actions. But, as we shall see, attempts to eliminate punishment from educational situations altogether fail. Punishment, though a nuisance, remains a useful and justifiable institution in society at large and in the school as well.

Learning from Consequences of Actions

Those who seek alternatives to punishment as measures to get children to comply with rules often argue that children should be confronted with the 'natural' or 'logical' consequences of their actions. Thus in one stroke it seems possible

1. to avoid the alleged repugnant practice of punishment, and
2. get children to learn and conform to necessary rules of conduct.

In his interesting article. 'On learning from the consequence of one's actions',[3] Tasos Kazepides argues that theorists such as Rousseau and Spencer of former times and, more recently, Rudolf Dreikurs and Harvey Clarizio, have mistakenly assumed that there are 'natural' or 'logical' consequences of action. Kazepides correctly argues that the terms 'natural consequences' and 'logical consequences' are at best otiose and substitutes for 'punishment' and at worst potential devices to camouflage manipulative teaching practices and failure in moral education. The problem with the notion of 'natural consequences' is that

1. either 'natural' rules out nothing, since whatever happens, happens in nature or is allowed by nature, or
2. it reflects someone's reasonable and ordinary (in that sense natural) but hidden prescription.

The problem with the notion of 'logical consequences' is that either

1. there are none, since the reference is really to societal, not logical rules, or
2. all the cases of 'logical' consequences are really cases of punishment, where it could be said that the punishment *really* fitted the crime.

The case of a teacher requiring a child to sit on a bench till he is ready to play is really a case of a teacher punishing a child for fooling around rather than the child learning from the 'logical' consequences of his actions. It is important that the action be viewed as punishment, for only as such is the teacher viewed as taking responsibility for his own action. The attempts by the 'consequence' theorists to interpret punishment in their terms is yet another attempt to escape the value judgment in education, yet another attempt to evade responsibility for the treatment of children, yet another failed attempt to reduce human volitional agency to mechanistic behaviourism. It is also a failed attempt to find a substitute for the use of punishment in dealing with children.

To have argued, as we have above, that there is a reasonable justification for the use of punishment in certain instances is not at all the same as having made a case for punitiveness, the view that the first and standard consideration in the treatment of children is punishment. Such a view is as unreasonable as the view that punishment should never be used. The tendency, as is often the case in education, is to go to one extreme or the other and evade the taxing responsibility of judging what is a reasonable position to take between the two extremes. The situation is similar to the problems surrounding the issues of freedom and authority in education.

Freedom and Authority

Because most people in Western democracies think that being free is a morally desirable state to be in, it is believed by many teachers and educational theorists that children should be prepared to be in that state by giving them as much freedom as possible and by refraining from exercising authority over them. This flies in the face of those who believe that there is insufficient law and order in the community and the school, that legitimate freedom is earned by acceptance of responsibility, and that exercise of authority over children is the route to such responsibility. And so the stage is set for yet another controversy in education. The central question in this controversy is whether authority can be justified while upholding the view that freedom is inherently a moral good. Part of the problem relates to the meaning of the terms 'freedom' and 'authority'. So, as usual, we will begin by providing conceptual clarification.

The Concept 'Freedom'

Despite masses of literature written on the concept 'freedom', it is really quite easily understood. Most of the problems centre on the justification for infringement on freedoms, which will be discussed later. Freedom essentially is a negative notion; it consists simply in doing what one wants to do without being interfered with by others. Because the restriction on freedom is so easily justified, the temptation is to write the restrictions into the notion of freedom itself. It is easy to argue that people are not free to bully, to steal, or to kill, for example; but that does not mean that accepted restrictions and a sense of responsibility must be logical conditions, that is, part of the meaning, of the notion of freedom. Legitimate restrictions on freedom are simply that, justified infringements on freedom.

Some writers, such as I. Berlin, argue that there are actually two notions of freedom extant.[4] In addition to the above negative notion is the concept of 'positive' freedom. In the negative concept there is reference to freedom *from* interference. In the 'positive' concept there is the notion of freedom *to* do things and want things; to have things and be somebody; to develop the capacities for enjoying things and performing at will. Development of positive freedom would be similar to developing those qualities, skills, and capacities characteristic of the educated person and similar to acquiring those benefits and materials characteristic of autonomous adults. The attraction in the notion of positive freedom is that it helps to account for such expressions commonly made as the 'freedom of having knowledge' or 'the freedom of being rich'. Also, in the context of education it can be argued that infringement on children's negative freedom can be justified on grounds of enhancing their positive freedom. But therein also lies one of the dangers in talking about positive freedom at all. According to some who oppose use of the term, there is no such thing as positive freedom. If we mean 'skill, capacity, ability, education, money' and so on, then we should name those things and not attempt to slide over the problem of justifying infringement on the only real freedom there is, namely negative freedom. Berlin himself warns us against tyrants who unwarrantably dominate over us in the name of positive freedom, who think authority over us is justified because we have not yet 'seen the light', as is evident by the fact that we still disagree with them. Such domination is not justified. Yet some infringements on 'negative' freedom are justified.

The Justification for Infringement on Freedom

In Chapter 7 of *Ethics and Education*, R.S. Peters argues that the principle of freedom is not merely an empirical condition, as proposed by utilitarians such as Mill, but a logical condition of morality. Its status as a moral principle is foundational and fundamental. As such, appeal to freedom need not be specifically justified against those who wish to infringe on it; rather the onus is always on those who want to interfere with freedom to provide good grounds. Such grounds are not difficult to establish or far to seek. We justify infringement on freedom on the grounds that there are other fundamental moral principles to satisfy — i.e., on grounds of justice, of equality, of prevention of harm and injury, of need for truth and keeping of promises and contracts. These general justifications by appeal to other moral principles are equally applicable in specific instances in schools. For reasons such as these, children are prohibited from bullying, stealing, interfering with and harming others, and so on. These are justified restrictions on pupil freedom in the context of behaviour in and about schools. But what about the justification for the denial of liberty that requires there to be a school context in the first place? When we send children to school we deny them freedom to remain at home. So the question of justification ranges from restrictions on individuals in their movement and behaviour to the larger issue of compulsory schooling itself.

But here too the justification for infringement is not far to seek. The most general form the justification takes is expressible in terms of the promotion of what is good for children. Two well-warranted assumptions behind this justification are:

1 that children by and large do not and cannot consistently want what is in their own interest and is good for them in the long run, and

2 that adults know better than children what is good for children.

Regarding the first assumption, children do indeed sometimes want what is good for them. They may want to study arithmetic, which is precisely what is good for them and what a teacher wants them to do. If so, there is of course, no issue about infringement on freedom. The point is rather that 'wanting' itself requires a certain amount of insight and education. Freedom to choose, when choosing means more than merely throwing dice, presupposes knowledge of alternatives and understanding of why one alternative is better than another. It is precisely because children do not yet have the sophisticated knowledge and understanding necessary to make choices about education that someone else must make these choices for them. The further assumption is that the things the children learn about would be objects of their wants if only they did know about them. Education deliberately changes or confirms certain wants in children in line with what is thought to be those things a child would choose if it could. In the long run, because the child will have more sophisticated and satisfying wants, the need for 'negative' freedom will be enhanced. So in terms of 'positive' and 'negative' freedom, there is a paradox. Freedom (negative) is denied so that freedom (positive) is enhanced, yielding greater freedom of both kinds in the long run.

The second assumption upon which justification for infringement on freedom rests is that adults know better than children what in the long run is good for children. For the justification to succeed, adults have to be right in this judgment. To have to make this judgment is no simple matter. It involves decisions about what constitutes the good life; it requires knowledge about children and about effects of teaching and pedagogical interventions; it demands a justification for education itself, such as will be entertained in Chapter 10. It is an awesome responsibility to have to make that judgment; and error is easily possible. Yet there is no escape in the human condition from some form of paternalism, despite fear of error and despite an appropriate attitude of humility. The question becomes one of who is in the best position to make the judgment. The answer to that is that those adults who have the highest degree of knowledge and experience in the relevant areas of consideration are most likely to make the fewest errors. They are experts or authorities who are socially sanctioned to infringe on children's right to freedom. Thus the justification for the use of authority in education runs parallel to the justification for infringement on freedom. A closer look at the nature of authority helps us to see why that is so.

The Nature of Authority

It is commonplace in philosophy of education literature to distinguish between being *in* authority and being *an* authority. Being in authority is to be placed in a socially sanctioned role, which carries with it certain rights and responsibilities. Being a bus driver, for example, gives one the right to demand that people sit or stay behind lines or not behave boisterously. The driver needs the power to enforce those rules so that he can fulfill his responsibility to get people safely and on time to their destinations. Appeals to challenges to authority are always to higher authorities, which if exhausted, end the appeal. Someone who is *an* authority is someone who is an expert in some area of knowledge or skill. Someone becomes *an* authority through study and practice. Challenge to such authority is appeal to evidence or reason. Therefore such authority is always provisional, depending on the best evidence available. It could happen, and eventually ideally should happen, that a teacher who is an authority will be superseded in knowledge by a student and the student thus becomes the authority. Even if that is so it does not follow that the teacher surrender his role *in* authority. The social role *can* be held even if it is not on the basis of superior knowledge and skill. If that does happen there are likely to be problems. Normally the reason people are placed *in* authority is that they are authorities on something. And so it is with teaching and, ideally, in the administration of education. A teacher obtains a job because of his acquired expertise in two areas: (1) in knowledge of subject matter, and (2) in pedagogical technique and theory.

A teacher ideally is an authority in authority. Because he is an authority he is equipped to make judgments about what and how children should learn. It is that capacity which places him in a role as teacher with the attendant power vested in him to force children, by rational means if at all possible, to submit to rules of a school and to curb their wants and deny them freedom. And if appeal to reason does not work he may, as someone in authority granted by the community, punish children if necessary tu conform to school rules and to accomplish school tasks. All this is justified in the name of education. But just because punishment, infringement of freedom, and use of power as someone in authority are justified under certain conditions, it does not follow that punitiveness, arbitrary interference, and authoritarianism are justified. Once again, the extreme position is the unreasonable one. Both authoritarianism, viewed as arbitrary exercise and love of power usually evident in too many and inflexible rules, as well as a complete *laissez-faire* attitude to behaviour, to academic standards, and to discipline are unwarranted extremes. The former is not permitted and the latter not required in education by the moral principle of freedom.

We see here some examples of a phenomenon in education that occurs frequently and is known as the paradox of education. The paradox can be stated as follows: an educational ideal the pursuit of which requires pedagogical action which seems to be a contradiction of the ideal. In the 'paradox of freedom' we thus observe the denial of freedom for the purpose of enhancing freedom. Other expressions of the paradox are: the route to autonomy is heteronomy; the road to independence, dependence; the achievement of enlightenment worthy of democracy, through non-democratic means. The same phenomenon will be evident in our study of moral education in the next chapter, where it will be observed that children are required to learn and obey moral rules before they can become independent in their moral reasoning. Consistent with this general paradox of education is the above-noted paradox of discipline, that is, learning self-discipline by having discipline first imposed externally. In similar manner authority over children is required so they can learn to live without it by becoming authorities themselves.

The teacher's position of authority is sometimes thought to be detrimental to the teaching situation because barriers between student and teacher are erected and the student becomes alienated from the school and the subject matter. This raises a number of interesting philosophical questions regarding the ideal student-teacher relationship, which will be the topic of discussion to conclude this chapter.

The Student-Teacher Relationship

In Chapter 6 of *The Logic of Education*, Hirst and Peters discuss two broadly-conceived types of student-teacher relationships: the role relationship and the personal relationship. Using that rough distinction we will in this section remark upon the advantages and disadvantages of the student-teacher relationship characterized in these two ways.

The Role Relationship

We have already noted that a teacher occupies a social role as a person in authority because he is an authority. The role has well-defined and limited rights and duties. Without exercising these rights and duties the task of teaching would become impossible. To speak of the relationship between teachers and students as a role-relationship is to suggest that the interchange between them be limited to those essential contacts required for the performance of duties for which the classroom was created, namely, teaching and learning. As such, the relationship would be characterized as impersonal. There would be little regard for an individual as a person other than what is necessary for the teaching and learning to occur. Because regard for individual pupil interests would be minimized, the class would likely be structured and rule-governed.

It cannot be taken for granted that to characterize a relationship as impersonal is automatically to condemn it. There are a number of advantages in conceiving of the student-teacher relationship as a role-relationship. First, there is removal of the stigma of anything untoward going on between the student and the teacher. There is a growing concern in recent years in some communities that children are being abused. Maintaining a role-relationship removes stigma from the teacher and fear from the student. Secondly, it is much easier to provide appropriate criticism of work done or of mis-behaviour when the relationship is not personal. Students expect teachers, but not friends, to criticize them. There is, thirdly, the advantage of the role-relationship enabling a teacher to avoid the disruptions of the inevitable liking and disliking of certain pupils. Favouritism is reduced and fairness advanced. Fourthly, the purposes of the school can more efficiently be achieved when the teacher and student focus on the subject matter rather than on each other as persons. This is an empirical assertion and may be somewhat overstated. Much depends on how much time and energy is devoted to cultivating personal relationship rather than maintaining the role-relationship. Fifthly, the demand that teachers extend their duties to cultivate personal relationship may be too emotionally and physically exhausting, leading to inevitable unfair distribution of attention and energy. Finally, it may well be that a relationship other than the role-relationship is of necessity too one-sided, leading to potential for manipulation and abuse.

Despite the above advantages of maintaining a strict role-relationship between teacher and student, there are obvious disadvantages. Most importantly is the deadening effect of impersonality in the interactions between student and teacher. Children are not merely subject-fodder, as Hirst and Peters so aptly point out; nor are teachers merely vehicles through whose heads ideas pass as they are transmitted from one generation to the next. The stultifying effect of alienation and distance between the student and the teacher as well as the subject-matter may render the whole educational engagement less effective and efficient than if a more personal approach is taken. That is why some educators stress the importance of personal relationships between teachers and students.

Personal Relationships

Personal relationships in general are those where two persons enter into reciprocal engagements. They share experiences; they divulge knowledge about themselves to each other; they cultivate common interests and reactions and so on. In the extreme form, there is no limit to the range of personal information shared and experiences enjoyed, which results eventually in complete intimacy.

Now when it is advocated that the student-teacher relationship be more personal, it is not being suggested that full personal relationships be entered into by everyone, but only that some of the characteristics of a personal relationship be adopted in addition to the role-relationship, leading to what Hirst and Peters call an 'embryonic personal relationship'.

There are a number of good reasons why the personal relationship is recommended. One advantage is that personal knowledge of the student helps the teacher in the task of appropriately displaying matter at a level where the student can learn. It will be remembered (see the section on 'The criteria for "teaching"' in Chapter 7) that one necessary condition of teaching is awareness of the student's cognitive level. To satisfy this, one must know something about the student as an individual. However, as Hirst and Peters point out, this does not take us very far toward a personal relationship. Even a monkey trainer needs to be aware of that much for successful training to occur. A more important consideration is the moral one, that students and teachers respect each other as persons. The moral requirement of respect for persons is this: 'In so far as we think of an individual as having a point of view, and in so far as this is not a matter of indifference to us, we respect him as a person'.[5] In a teaching situation this demand for respect goes beyond merely awareness of the cognitive level of the learner, but must include consideration of others' point of view, of their pride and aspirations, and of their feelings and sensitivities. A further advantage in the personal relationship is that showing personality (by the teacher) can be a motivating device for students. If the students observe the teacher overcoming difficulty, frustration, and weariness, they are more likely to do so as well; for modelling is a more effective pedagogical technique when mutual respect is evident. Still another advantage to the personal relationship is that it satisfies the demands that the teacher be a moral educator, both by way of precept and example. Teaching how to conduct personal relationships might well be one of the responsibilities of the teacher. Therefore to show care and concern for individual persons in the classroom is to fulfil a duty as a model of moral, as well as non-moral, virtues. The kinds of embryonic personal relationship between student and teacher, as advocated by Hirst and Peters, strike a balance between the two extremes. It avoids the alienating effect of impersonality and still maintains the distance necessary to carry out the teaching and learning task for which the encounter between teacher and student was undertaken in the first place.

Suggested further readings:

BERLIN, I. (1969) 'Two concepts of liberty' in *Four Essays on Liberty*, Oxford University Press, pp. 118–172.

HIRST, P.H. and PETERS, R.S. (1970) *The Logic of Education*, London, Routledge and Kegan Paul, 'Discipline and punishment', pp. 124–31; and 'Teaching and personal relationships', pp. 88–105; and 'Authority and educational institutions', pp. 113–24.

KAZEPIDES, T. (1978) 'On learning from the consequences of one's action' in *Oxford Review of Education*, 4, pp. 77–84.

PETERS, R.S. *Ethics and Education*, op. cit., 'Punishment and discipline', pp. 266–290; and 'Authority and education', pp. 237–265.

Notes

1 See *The Logic of Education*, op. cit., p. 126.
2 See section on 'Inaptness of the organic metaphor' in Chapter 2 of this book.
3 In *Oxford Review of Education*, 4, 1, 1978, pp. 77–83.
4 See BERLIN, I. (1969) 'Two concepts of liberty' in his *Four Essays on Liberty*, Oxford, Chapter 3.
5 HIRST, P.H. and PETERS, R.S. (1970) op. cit., p. 92.

Questions and Exercises

Answer the following questions as briefly as possible (two or three sentences should suffice in most instances):
1 How is discipline different from punishment?
2 What are the necessary conditions for 'punishment'? Can the innocent be punished?
3 Must punishment be retributive?
4 Distinguish between being an authority, being in authority and being authoritarian?
5 What is the meaning of 'free'?
6 Is the ability to do something a necessary condition of being free to do it? How would you describe a lack of ability to do something which you might want to do but can't?
7 What is the distinction between 'positive' and 'negative' freedom?

8 Why is the notion of positive freedom frowned upon by some philosophers?

9 What is the general justification for a teacher infringing on a student's right to freedom?

10 What problems result if human beings are left to learn only from the 'natural' consequences of their actions?

Answer the following questions in a paragraph or two.

1 Can education occur without discipline? Without punishment? What is the logical connection between discipline and education?

2 What are the general grounds (or justification) for the use of punishment? Are the same grounds satisfactory for the use of punishment in educational contexts?

3 'At least sometimes someone else knows better than you do what is good for you or what is in your interest to do or pursue.' Do you agree with that statement? Why or why not? What are the implications of your position for education?

CHAPTER 9

Moral Education

Introduction: Why Moral Education?

Why should the public school be concerned with moral education at all? Part of the answer is that parents and society at large consider it extremely important that new members of society behave properly. Their own well-being is affected by the way children are reared and socialized. Usually parents and the public shy away from terms such as 'moral' or 'ethical', believing these to be too private and controversial for the school to be concerned with. (We shall see below why this is not so). They express their concern more comfortably with terms such as 'sociability', 'good citizenship', 'character development', 'cooperation', 'need for discipline', and similar expressions. These concerns are often the very ones which below are described as social moral concerns and lie at the heart of moral education. The fact that parents have such a strong concern and that moral education has once again become very topical in educational circles and educational research in the last few decades is only one reason why moral education should be the concern of the public schools. Even if moral education were not popular, it can well be maintained that it has been and cannot but be a central issue in education regardless of popularity or recognition. It is inconceivable that moral values such as truthfulness, fair treatment, thoughtfulness for others and so on could be disregarded or excluded from any social group but particularly groups concerned with rearing children. But there is an even stronger argument for inclusion of morality in education; and that is because morality is, as was argued in Chapters 3 and 4, a form of knowledge without which a well-rounded education, and therefore also fully developed person, is impossible. Assuming that the school's role is primarily education, it follows that the school must also be concerned with moral education.

Moral Education and Values Education

One of the reasons why moral education is so controversial is that it is often mistakenly used as meaning values education in general. But if 'moral education' and 'values education' are used inter-changeably and synonymously it is no wonder that confusion arises and that people become concerned about the appropriateness of moral education in the public school. For if personal preferences and private tastes are being foisted on others in the name of education, there are indeed good grounds to object. But, of course, only one small subset of values are moral values. In fact one of the very first steps in coming to understand the nature of moral education is to sort out the kinds of values there are and spot within the broad spectrum that area of values which is the legitimate domain of moral education. Such a sorting out is still far from complete and satisfactory in the philosophical literature. The two diagrams to follow represent different ways of approaching the problem of classifying values. The first one (Table 3) is based on the work of Hamm and Daniels[1]; the second (Table 4) attempts further to isolate moral values from other values.

The third diagram in the series (Table 5) represents a more detailed working out of moral values themselves. It forms the subject matter of moral education in its entirety, at least as far as moral education is conceived of in this book. A case can be made for there being a kind of personal morality, having to do with self-development, personal integrity, and individual authenticity[2]; but this chapter will be exclusively concerned with inter-personal, social morality. We are here considering as morality only those rules and principles which govern relations between people. The subtitle for Table 5 is therefore 'social moral values'; and the discussions below on approaches to moral education are to be taken exclusively within the context of social moral education.

Moral Development as the Achievement of Virtue

Moral education literature and research present a confused picture to parents or school teachers concerned with the day-to-day task of

Table 3: Kinds of values (First Attempt)

Class A	Class B	Class C
— distinguishable logical structure	— basic needs and wants residing in human nature	— individual preferences
— objective (inter-subjective)	— universal (or nearly so)	— matter of habit and custom
— intrinsically valuable for any rational being	— objective (partially)	— local or private in character
— presupposed for all rational thought and discourse	— instrumental to pursuit of good life	— arbitrary (to a degree)
— necessary part of moral discourse		— lack rational justification
— rule governed		— idiosyncratic

Class A		Class B	Class C	
A₁ *Non-normative*	A₂ *Normative*	— health and physical well-being	*Local Group Values*	*Private Values*
		— freedom from pain		
Logic	Aesthetics	— social well-being	— manners	— style of dress
Mathematics	Morals	— loyalty	— conventions	— choice of friends
Physical and Nat. Science	Political Theory	— legality	— local rules of operation	— food preferences
Social Sciences	Religion?	— order		— choice of occupation
History		— predictability (institutions)		— choice of recreation
Philosophy		— citizenship (belonging)		— conflict of moral

Underlying procedural principles for all rational thought ('rational passions')
— clarity
— consistency
— open-mindedness
— relevance
— coherence
— precision
— parsimony
  (Occam's Razor)

— security and safety
—— absence of fear
—— absence of threat and danger
—— absence of frustration
—— economic well-being
— friendship and association
—— fraternity
—— intimacy
—— familiarity
— vocational success
— sexual fulfillment

Derivative Class B Values
thrift, industriousness, loyalty, perseverence, orderliness, prudence, cleanliness, courage

values (dilemma)
— lifestyles (limited by morality)
— religious values
— sexual expression
— entertainment
— 'environmental' ethic (also local group value)

Table 4: Kinds of values (Second Attempt)

A. Moral	B. Non-Moral	
1 Justice (equality, fairness, impartiality)	**1 Subjective**	**2 Objective**
	a. Where two moral values conflict (e.g., freedom, equality)	a. Aesthetic (fine arts)
2 Feedom		(i) literature
		(ii) music
	b. Dress	(iii) art — pictorial — sculpture
3 Beneficence	c. Occupations (limited by morality)	(iv) movement
		(v) architecture
4 Non-Maleficence (non-injury)	d. Life styles (limited by morality to a degree only)	b. Health and physical well-being
5 Truthfulness (contract and promise keeping)	e. Sexual expression (limited by moral considerations)	c. Social stability (political) — loyalty — legality — citizenship

     — order, predictability
     — institutions

d. Security and safety
     — absence of fear
     — eradication of danger
     — elimination of frustration
     — economic

e. Rationality leading to autonomy
     — pursuit of truth
     — pursuit of knowledge in various forms (science, history, etc.)

f. Friendship and association
     — fraternity
     — intimacy

f. Religious values

g. Smells, tastes (literally)

h. Recreation

i. Games

Table 5: Kinds of moral values (Social Moral Values)

Fundamental Principles	Derived Principles	Rules
1 Justice (fairness, equality, impartiality)	— No discrimination on basis of irrelevant differences such as colour, race, creed, sex, etc. — Equality of opportunity	— Form queue — Take turns — Don't talk out of turn — Don't hog conversation — Don't take what isn't yours — Obey impartial judges (e.g., umpire, parent, teacher)
2 Freedom	— Of press, speech, thought — Of assembly — Of religion — From threat, anxiety	— Don't bully — Leave others alone — Don't interfere — Respect others' privacy — Don't use or manipulate people — Don't coerce or force others

3 Beneficence	— Consideration of others' interests	— Don't be selfish, greedy
	— Consideration of minority interests	— Help others in need
	— Maintain human life and health	— Don't insult or degrade others
	— Protect the weak (e.g., children, handicapped)	— Be kind
		— Be thoughtful of others
		— Be generous
4 Non-Maleficence	— Minimize pain	— Don't physically or mentally hurt others
	— Don't injure persons	— Don't fight
	— Don't harm others	— Don't be mean
		— Don't steal
		— Don't damage property
		— Don't mess needlessly
5 Truthfulness	— Keep contracts	— Don't cheat
	— Keep promises	— Don't lie
	— Present evidence	— Don't 'cook' the evidence
	— No indoctrination	— Don't deceive
		— Don't be a hypocrite

rearing children. Models of moral education vying for public acceptability — models such as Kohlberg's cognitive moral development, Raths' values clarification, Shaver's rationale building model, McPhail's lifeline model, Newman's social action model, Coombs's value analysis model, Bech's reflective approach, Wilson's proceduralism — are sometimes too complex and difficult to put into practice, sometimes too narrow (or alternatively too broad) in scope to reflect a justifiable conception of morality, and sometimes expressed in a language too technical or unclear for practitioners to grasp easily. They are also often at cross-purposes. All of these models have positive as well as negative features, some decidedly more so than others. But this is not the place for a full-scale analysis and appraisal of these models, which has in any case been done elsewhere.[3] (Below we will examine very briefly only two such models). What is needed is a new model which is clear and comprehensive, theoretically and practically sound, taking into account the well-known strengths and weaknesses of these other models, and expressed in a language easily understood by theorists and practitioners alike. That is what is being presented in this chapter. With the availability of such a model it is not necessary for harried and confused teachers (or other practitioners) to grasp at and embrace one of many other such models more or less arbitrarily because they don't know where else to turn.

Developmentalism and Values Clarification Rejected

An example of a model that is too narrow in scope as well as theoretically and scientifically suspect and yet continues to be embraced by researchers and practitioners, is Kohlberg's theory of moral development.[4] For the last several decades Kohlberg has had a significant influence on the practice of moral education in schools as well as a profound influence on how moral education is conceived. Many have questioned the value of his influence. In a paper entitled 'On assessing Kohlberg's stage theory of moral development', Nicolayev and Phillips undertake a thorough examination of the scientific adequacy of Kohlberg's research into children's moral development. They conclude that, 'in the light of the available evidence, there is good reason for believing that the hard core of the Kohlbergian research programme is implausible'.[5] Despite this observation, they argue that, since it is imperative that moral reasoning continue to be studied, the Kohlbergian research should not be abandoned. They note:

Research programs in important areas cannot be abandoned, regardless of their weakness, until alternatives are available. Research is directionless unless it is guided by some hypothesis or heuristic device; and possibly anything is better than nothing. If there were a rival research program in the same field, however, one of the chief reasons for continuing to embrace Kohlberg would disappear.[6]

Kohlberg has been criticized not only for his lack of adequacy in scientific methodology but also for his failure to conceptualize moral education adequately. His almost exclusive concern with justice leaves untouched the need to investigate how children acquire judgment with respect to other moral principles such as truthfulness and beneficence. Furthermore, Kohlberg has been concerned almost exclusively with children's judgment as distinct from their moral behaviour, a problem that will be alluded to again below. Also to be touched on later is the problem of Kohlberg's pedagogical technique of presenting dilemmas rather than teaching content in the form of rules and principles. For all these reasons Kohlberg's approach has been deemed too narrow and too empirically suspicious.

Nicolayev's and Phillips's reluctance to abandon Kohlberg rests on their assumption that no alternative heuristic device is available to constitute a rival research programme. In this chapter that assumption is challenged by an attempt to construct such a rival model. Whether the model will yield a paradigm easily amenable to scientific research is, however, not guaranteed. This is because the model is not merely the construction of a paradigm for scientific research, but a comprehensive model which includes an articulation and justification of what constitutes morality and a description of the criterion of success in moral education as well as a set of procedures for bringing it about. The model, in other words, has a philosophical component as well as psychological and sociological ones; and the building of the model, because it draws on several disciplines, exemplifies an exercise in educational theory. And here, as elsewhere in educational theory, the necessity for scientific investigation may recede in significance in favour of common-sense strategies once the objectives of the exercise are clearly spelled out. Indeed, the view here taken is that once the content of morality is carefully spelled out — that is, once the criterion of success is pinpointed — matters concerning strategy quickly fall into place. That is why the philosophical component is still the central and most important area of investigation into moral education. In any case, ease of scientific investigation should not dictate what will count as moral education objectives (perhaps the problem with Kohlberg); rather, scientific investigation must conform to the requirements of a philosophically sound model. Good argument, *not* amenability to scientific investigation, justifies moral education objectives.

An example of a model that is empirically suspect and conceptually confused because it is too broad in scope is the approach to (moral?) education known as values clarification.[7] Though this model potentially has some merits (openness for discussion purposes, non-threatening environment, therapeutic value, diagnostic potential, encouragement of thought about consequences of action), it is, despite its contemporary wide acceptance by teachers, seriously flawed to the extent that it is possibly more damaging than helpful as a technique of moral education. Not only is there little evidence that it works as moral education and that it lessens value confusion, it also is theoretically problematic (having an inadequate concept of values and being internally inconsistent), lacks a modelling effect, confuses many sorts of values, presents no tools for examining values, is parasitic on others' teaching insofar as positive effects are forthcoming, and worst of all subscribes to extreme relativism in ethics to the extent that children who have begun to get a good grasp of justifiable moral principles are taught that all values, including social moral values, are just a matter of taste. For these and other reasons the model is rejected in favour of what is here referred to as the virtues approach to moral education.

The construction of a new model, then, begins with a theoretical basis for moral education in which the nature of morality is described and objectives for moral education are isolated. Thereafter three elements of a procedural nature are separately explained and discussed. On the basis of these procedural elements some strategies are suggested. Also, some conclusions are drawn for teacher education and for further research.

Theoretical Bases for a Model of Moral Education

A sound model of moral education must have a sound theory of morality in terms of which moral education objectives can be formulated. So the first task is to make clear what morality is, or at least how it is conceived of in this model. This is not easy to do simply and quickly; but it must be done if we are to achieve our goal. Perhaps the best way to begin is to say what morality is not.

First, morality is not merely a description of the behavioural patterns and practices of a group, such as a sociologist might discover in studying the mores of a particular society. Of any such practices or mores it is possible to ask, and people do ask, 'But ought such practices to exist? Are they right and good?' In other words the moral judgment comes in after the description of the practices is made; and to observe this is to observe an important feature of morality, namely, that moral judgments, at least some of them and the most important of them, are cross-cultural and universal, appealing as they do to standards outside any particular culture. It follows from this observation also that some researchers who study the processes of socialization of children or those who study causes of anti-social behaviour may not in fact be studying processes of moral education at all, even if it is alleged that they are. It depends on whether the practices into which people are socialized are moral or not. It is possible for socialized behaviour to be immoral and for moral behaviour to be anti-social.

Secondly, morality is not necessarily conformity to religious, political, or legal prescriptions. Moral education models that attempt to substitute religious education or political education or legal education for moral education may be missing the mark in the same way that mere socialization may miss the mark. That is not to say that the institutions of religion, politics, and the law are necessarily anti-moral; fortunately they often underline and encourage moral behaviour and enhance moral understanding in their teachings. But it is to say that they are not *necessarily* moral; and from the moral standpoint they must conform to the demands of moral reason when they conflict with its requirement. These observations highlight two further features of morality. One is that morality, as a form of human discourse and thought, is autonomous; its demands are not dependent on, or reducible to, any other form of thought or discourse. The other feature is that the demands of morality are overriding; no prescription from any other form of discourse can for a rational person in normal circumstances take precedence.

Thirdly, morality is not a form of rational prudence. It is sometimes thought that because an individual wisely arranges his life in such a way as to fulfil his personal ideals for the good life, he has achieved morality. Such a person will be likely to have worked hard to get a good job, have sufficient income and a sizeable pension, not waste or gamble, will obey the law and conform to social practices to avoid social friction, set great store in pursuing literature and the arts, treasure excellence in sports and other leisure-time activities, perfect his talents, fulfil his potential, and so on. Such a person is said to have his values in order. Here, as has been argued elsewhere,[8] there is a sense in which the pursuit of personal values has a moral dimension. There is a language of worth expressing judgements about how one ought to live one's life quite apart from how it affects others. But this form of personal morality, or morality of the good life, must be sharply distinguished from social morality, where rules governing behaviour are entirely of the inter-personal regulatory kind. It needs to be noted that we are here concerned exclusively with the latter. The model of moral education is a model of social or inter-personal moral education, as has already been mentioned.

So far we have remarked only on what morality is not; it is time now to try to give an account of what it is. To begin with it will be asserted, leaving it until later to explain the reasonableness of the assertion, that morality is doing the right thing for the right reason and moral education is getting others to do the right thing for the right reason. Now an astute reader will immediately question this assertion by pointing out that sometimes we can do the right thing (place a cross-court smash) for the right reason (frustrate the opponent and win the game) and not be within the moral domain at all. The objection is a good one; but the reply to that is that what is really meant is that we should do the *morally* right thing for the *morally* right reason. The astute reader will press on with his objection by noting that the claim now is circular. Again he is right; but the circularity is not of a vicious kind, as philosophers would say, because it highlights the point already made, that morality is autonomous. No reason of a non-moral kind will satisfy the demands of morality. A little later we will explain what makes a reason a moral one. For now it will simply be noted that doing the right thing for the right reason is a necessary condition, though not a sufficient one, for morality; and as such it points to two further features of morality.

One is that morality is centrally concerned with the giving of reasons. The terms 'should', 'ought', and their cognates are the standard terms used to make moral injunctions. The almost automatic and correct response to, 'You ought to do so and so', is 'Why?', suggesting that moral judgments are not merely expressing feelings but are based on supporting reasons. And it is because there are available publicly acceptable, objective reasons for moral judgments, based, as we shall see, on universal principles, that it is appropriate to speak of moral *education* proper, as distinct from training, where 'education' implies knowledge and understanding and getting 'on the inside of a form of thought'.[9] The other point to note is that morality requires not only good judgment but also corresponding action; to be fully moral one must *do* the right thing as well as have the right reason. Both are required. It takes into account two prominent themes in moral theory — the emphasis on motive and reason as promulgated by Kant and the emphasis on good consequences as emphasized by utilitarians such as Mill. It also corresponds to our common understanding of moral behaviour. The reason or motive one has for doing a particular act changes the character of the act. To drive a car slowly and cautiously midst a crowd or past a playground because one has noticed a policeman in the rear-vision mirror does not count as a moral act; whereas if one does so to prevent possible harm to people, irrespective of the presence of a patrol or a law requiring it, then it does count as a moral act. In one sense, of course, the act was the same; the car was driven slowly. But that is merely to say that one can do the right thing for the wrong reason or for no reason; just as one can also do the wrong thing for the wrong reason or fail to do the right thing despite having the right reasons.

These are all various forms of moral turpitude. And there are obviously good social reasons why it is better to do the right thing for the wrong reason or no reason, rather than not doing the right thing at all. It may in fact be that children do, and must, begin their moral education in that manner, as we shall see. Nevertheless it is only when one does the right thing for the right reason that one has fully achieved morality. How the actor views his action makes all the difference from a moral standpoint. Now a third person observed may not see a difference in the two acts of driving slowly. An impartial scientist who studies only observable phenomena may have a problem here in properly describing the two actions because the motive is not observable. He may then have much less to contribute to the understanding and explanation of moral phenomena than is sometimes thought. Furthermore, what counts as a moral reason is not subject to scientific investigation. That is why it was noted earlier that a model of moral education which includes an adequate description of the nature of morality may find in it a lesser role for scientific investigation than is often assumed.

But to return to our main concern. We have said that morality is concerned with the giving of reasons, but we left open the question of why certain reasons are moral ones and others not. What then is the nature of *moral* reasons? Quite obviously some reasons for action are not moral, even if they are genuinely my reasons.

Someone who says that one should be kind because it is sunny and it is Thursday is not giving moral reasons, because such reasons are not relevant to morality. A reason such as 'because it relieves suffering' is relevant. For *my* reasons to be moral, they must be *the* relevant moral reasons. But what makes reasons relevant? Reasons are relevant if they appeal to certain moral principles, which are referred to as constituent fundamental principles. And what are these? What is their source? How does one justify them? To answer these questions takes us to the heart of moral philosophy, for which there is here little space. But it is possible briefly to describe how they are arrived at, and not difficult to state what they are. Their source derives from some observations of the human condition together with considerations about what makes rational behaviour possible. There is near-universal agreement that mankind has in common a set of fears, if realized, and wants, if not realized, that makes the human condition quite intolerable. L.M. Loring says:

> We believe, or we take it for granted, that besides immediate pain, such experiences as fear and frustration are universally disagreeable, and that the sense of physical well-being, confidence, and the ability to do what we want to do are universally agreeable. This body of ideas, so much part of our human thinking that it usually passes unnoticed, I call 'the basic values assumption'.[10]

This 'basic values assumption' forms one objective basis for moral principles. The occasion for morality is that people live in groups and that conflict of interests is unavoidable. The point and purpose of morality is, in G.J. Warnock's terms, 'to ameliorate the human predicament'[11] through the use of reason (rather than by other measures such as force, or manipulation, or replenishment of resources) when human interests conflict. The use of reason in this predicament requires that certain other principles be posited because they are logically required for reason to operate. Generalizability and the principles of justice and equality, for example, are presupposed in what makes a reason a reason. If one considers the point and purpose of morality, together with the logically necessary conditions presupposed for moral discourse to be possible, one is able to provide a fairly complete set of constitutive moral principles acceptable to, and widely accepted by, any rational person, such principles being both formal enough to catch the essence of the unique character of moral discourse and rich enough in substance to provide guidance in practical inter-personal behaviour and judgment. These principles can briefly be stated as follows:

1   Justice as fairness, often expressed in terms such as impartiality, non-arbitrariness, moral equality, and non-discrimination.
2   Non-maleficence, enjoining restraint from harming or injuring others.
3   Minimal beneficence, so phrased to indicate our responsibility to assist others in satisfying their basic needs, though not the obligation to satisfy all wants envisaged in conceptions of a good life.
4   Freedom, the injunction that without justification we have no right to interfere with others doing what they want to do.
5   Honesty, expressible also as truthfulness and non-deception.

These principles are not only necessary but, arguably, also sufficient for inter-personal morality. They constitute the foundation of morality. Any reason that derives from these principles is a relevant moral reason. If a reason does not appeal to these principles directly or indirectly, then the reason is irrelevant from a moral standpoint. A number of secondary principles are derivable from each of the fundamental ones, and from each of the secondary principles one can derive a host of moral rules which provide specific guides for action. Examples of derived principles are: do not discriminate on the basis of colour, race, sex, or creed differences; provide equal opportunity; avoid denial of freedom of press, speech, thought, and assembly; consider minority interests; maintain health and life; protect the weak and ill; minimize pain; don't injure or harm others; keep contracts and promises; present evidence; don't indoctrinate. Examples of lower-level derivative rules are: take turns; form a queue; don't talk out of turn; don't hog the conversation; don't take what isn't yours; don't bully; don't needlessly interfere; don't manipulate others; respect others' privacy; don't be selfish or greedy; don't insult or degrade others; be kind and thoughtful; be generous; don't fight; don't damage property; don't mess needlessly; don't cheat, lie, or cook the evidence; don't deceive or be a hypocrite; be sincere. And with a little bit of thought the list could go on and on.

Above we noted that the principles from which these rules derive stem from 'considerations about what makes rational behaviour possible'.[12] It is these 'rational' conditions for morality that need to be elaborated on briefly here to provide further insight into the foundations of morality. In this argument we will closely follow the work of R.S. Peters in his *Ethics and Education*. Peters argues that the justification of moral principles can best proceed by using a 'Kantian-type' argument. He then describes this procedure as a 'form of justification of principles consist(ing) of probing behind them in order to make explicit what they implicitly presuppose'.[13] Or again: 'If it could be shown that certain principles are necessary for a form of discourse to have meaning, to be applied, or to have point, then this would be a very strong argument for the justification of the principles in question'.[14] To illustrate how this argument works we will examine how he demonstrates that the principle of justice is a criterial attribute of morality, or, what is the same thing, that justice is presupposed in any attempt to justify conduct. The bare skeleton of the argument is as follows:

(a) The question 'why ought I to do X?' is a typical request for moral advice or moral justification.

(b) Why ought I to do X?' presupposes choice between alternatives. Otherwise there would be no point in asking the question seriously.

(c) Considering alternatives (a logical requirement of choice) presupposes discriminable differences between situations constituting grounds or reasons for action. Otherwise there would be no point or meaning in considering alternatives.

(d) Adducing reasons presupposes impartiality. Reasons, that is to say, are by their very nature such that they create categories stipulating relevant and irrelevant considerations. If this were not so there would be no point in adducing reasons.

(e) Impartiality presupposes general rules that make reasons relevant. No answer to the question 'Why ought I?' is better or worse than any other unless there are principles for accepting or rejecting reasons on relevant grounds.

(f) The notion of general rules presupposes the general notion of no distinction without differences. That is, the notion of general rules presupposes 'that what ought to be done in any particular situation or by any particular person ought to be done in any other situation or by another person unless there is some relevant difference in the situation or person in question' (p.122). If this were not so quoting general rules would have no point or meaning.

(g) The general notion of no distinction without differences is the general principle of rationality exemplified in situations of practical reasoning. This principle is applied in various specific contexts when we judge people, actions, or choices as impartial, fair, or simply just. Justice, as well as impartiality, fairness, and equality, are thus demonstrated as resting on this fundamental principle of morality. To refuse to accept this general principle is to refuse to engage in any attempt at justifying conduct, which is tantamount to a refusal to engage in moral discourse.

Peters goes on in *Ethics and Education* using a similar type of argument to establish, with greater or lesser effectiveness, four other fundamental principles, *viz.*, worthwhileness of certain activities, consideration of others' interest, freedom, and respect for persons. For our present purposes it is not necessary to examine each of these arguments individually. What has been attempted is just to illustrate the kind of argument usable in different forms to justify positing the principles mentioned which are constitutive of moral thought, and without which rational morality would be impossible.

If the above is correct, then, because these rules and principles can be cited as relevant moral reasons, we can satisfy the demand that moral action requires right reasons. If children are to be morally educated they will somehow have to acquire an understanding of these rules and principles and learn to employ them in making moral judgments. But more is required; they will also have to acquire the disposition to act according to their understanding. They must *do* the right thing as well as have the right reasons. These two aspects of morality correspond to William Frankena's[15] claim that moral education consists of both (1) handing on of moral knowledge about good and evil, of knowing how to act (and this can be conceived of as moral education proper), and (2) ensuring that children's conduct will conform to this knowledge (and this can be conceived of as moral training, if the appellation 'education' in this context seems out of place). Both in any case are required. They are required for moral reasons as well as pragmatic and pedagogical reasons. The moral reason is rather obvious. To have moral knowledge without putting it into practice defeats the main point and purpose of morality which is to ameliorate the human predicament. In fact it is a severe form of moral turpitude to know and not do. But more than this. According to some views, the doing must stem from the appropriate attitude or disposition. Aristotle depicts the virtuous person thus:

> We may use the pleasure (or pain) that accompanies the exercise of our dispositions as an index of how far they have established themselves. A man is temperate who abstaining from bodily pleasures finds this abstinence pleasant; if he finds it irksome, he is intemperate.[16]

In other words the morally educated person is one who acts according to the right reason habitually or, as we say, by second nature. And this accords with our experience when we observe that something is morally amiss in someone, say a teacher, who, each time he picks up a student's exam paper, must stop and assess whether he should mark it fairly or not. However, it seems that this is not a logical necessity, but a pragmatic one. Purely on logical grounds it would seem that a person could not be faulted for carefully thinking through every move he ever made to check for moral correctness, except perhaps that he would not get much done in the world as it is. Rather, it seems, we reduce to habit most of our actions because it is demanded by practical living. It simplifies life. Only in new and difficult situations do we bring to bear the full logic of moral reasoning. So it is still important for non-moral reasons that acting according to moral rules should become part of our disposition. It is important too for pedagogical reasons. Children can and must behave appropriately long before they are able to reason morally; so here again it is necessary that good behaviour be made dispositional. It is for the above reasons that the notion of virtue is introduced. A virtue, as in here used and as reflected in ordinary usage, is the disposition to behave according to a morally justified rule or principle. What makes a particular human quality a virtue is how well a morally acceptable practice (based on whether or not it is an instance of a moral principle), has become internalized as a feature of one's character. A person may be said to have the virtue honesty if he has learnt to be honest; and whether he views honesty as a practice required by others or as a practice required by appeal to fundamental moral principles does not detract from his having that virtue. What matters is that honesty be morally justified and that it become dispositional. Thus the notion of virtue fits both the cases of (1) someone, usually a child, who, on his way to becoming morally educated, is dispositionally honest while progressively acquiring a fuller understanding of and justification for honesty, and (2) someone who is honest because he has fully understood and justified for himself the importance of honesty. It is for these reasons that the model here presented might be called, 'the virtues approach' to moral education.

How the achievement of virtue is accomplished we shall turn to in the following sections. Before that, however, it is necessary to comment and expand on two points in explanation and elaboration of the above description of the theoretical bases for moral education.

Remarks on the teaching of moral content
The subject-matter, or the cognitive component, of social moral education is quite simple and straightforward. There just is no substance to claims such as Kohlberg's that 'there are no moral virtues'.[17] The rules forming the bases for virtues are few, simple, specific, and clear. Why then is there such reluctance on the part of moral educators to acknowledge that and proceed to teach specific moral content? The standard objections to the teaching of moral content include the following: (1) the content is situation specific, not universal, and since there is no agreement on content the teaching of it amounts to an unjustified imposition of partisan values; and so (2) teaching content leaves no room for relativity in ethics; (3) the teaching of content, because it does not provide reason for rules, amounts to indoctrination; and (4) the teaching of content shows lack of respect for children because it denies children autonomy in ethics.

However, none of these objections seems to be justified. The disagreement in ethics, while it might apply more to personal morality, is far less serious with respect to social moral rules and principles than is sometimes supposed. In any case, it is not on the basis of agreement that one justifies these rules and principles; it is rather a question of whether they are justifiable on rational grounds. If a segment of society does not agree that honesty is a virtue, we simply have no moral reason or justification for accommodating to that view, since it is irrational to do so. Truth in ethics is not decided democratically any more than is truth in science. So, at the fundamental level at least, there is no room for relativity of social moral principles. At the level of local rules, however, there is room in this model for limited, legitimate relativity. Depending on the facts in a specific situation, two local rules can be at variance, in fact can be perfectly contrary, and still both subscribe to a single universally justified principle or rule. The rule 'Bath frequently' promulgated in a context where water is plentiful, disease and odours are rampant, and so on, and the rule 'Bath infrequently' promulgated in a context where there is hardly enough water to drink, and so on, are both justified on the same grounds: be thoughtful of others' interests and be fair. So the content as outlined above accommodates the required relativity. With respect to the charge of indoctrination, much depends on what one takes indoctrination to be. On the view (which in this work is held to be correct) that indoctrination is a process of teaching doctrines, where doctrines are held to be beliefs for which no conceivable sort of counter-evidence is allowable, then the teaching of content is not indoctrination because the content is justified in terms of the principles from which they derive, and the principles themselves are rationally justified. If one takes the view that indoctrination is primarily to be analyzed in terms of method of instruction, then the objection is not really against content as such, but against certain ways in which content is taught. Later we shall see that content can be taught in such a way as to allow reasons to be given; so that the charge of indoctrination can be entirely neutralized. Nor does the teaching of content disrespect children by denying them legitimate autonomy. The claim that in morals children must be allowed to choose freely, as demanded by autonomy, is ambiguous. Wilson, for example, insists on the 'importance of pupils' moral beliefs being *their* own beliefs'[18] (his emphasis). This could mean at least two things. It could mean, on the one hand, that children should come to accept for themselves moral rules that are justified and justifiable for anyone and everyone on public rational grounds, in which case they achieve autonomy in the sense of being genuine and authentic and not merely responding to the rules in a second-hand or artificial manner. By seeing the point of the rules they acquire the strength of will in the face of counter-inclination. On the other hand it could mean that children should, to satisfy the demands of autonomy, make up or arrive at moral rules that are uniquely their own rules. Now it is the former, not the latter, that is required by rational morality. In the sphere of social morality there just is not much legitimate room for choice of content. The demands of reason severely limit the choice of social moral content. Telfer remarks: 'Many duties to others are exceedingly cut and dried and admit of no uncertainty as to whether a breach has taken place'.[19] One can conclude, then, that the standard objections to the teaching of content are ill-founded. If that is correct, it should have the effect of removing reluctance to teach content.

Remarks on the pedagogical use of the moral dilemma
As is obvious from our previous enumeration of five constitutive

fundamental principles, morality makes multiple demands. It is multifold and pluralistic, not singular and monistic in conception. This view of morality is now widely accepted. But on the basis of this view it is also widely believed and asserted that the availability of rules and principles is of little help in solving standard moral problems because the multiplicity of principles and rules leads to inevitable conflict in application, and so there is after all no agreement possible in moral judgment. Therefore it would also be false and foolhardy to teach children that these rules can be applied in a consistent and uncomplicated way. As a consequence of holding such a view, most moral education theorists and researchers focus on the dilemma in which moral principles clash as the typical case of a moral problem. Moral education on this view amounts to a strategy for helping children wriggle out of moral dilemmas. Emphasis is on developing a form of thinking rather than on teaching content. As is well known, Kohlberg's examples for children to contemplate are exclusively dilemmas. Modelling after Kohlberg, R.A. Milne, in 'Moral Development in Early Childhood',[20] uses, for purposes of studying children's moral thinking, an example in which two children arrive at the swing at the same time and must work out who goes first. Now this almost exclusive concern with the moral dilemma, it is here contended, is a serious mistake. This point needs to be emphasized. It is my claim that both moral theorists and moral education theorists have seriously misled us by using the moral dilemma as the paradigm of a moral problem, suggesting as it does that moral rules and principles cannot in the final analysis guide moral judgment and therefore leave moral reasoning impotent and moral judgment arbitrary. To explain and elaborate this contention, let us consider three moral situations.

(a) Johnny is opposite the lolly counter thinking he can take some candy without being caught. He knows it is wrong to steal; but doesn't want to spend his money if he can get away with it. His heart is racing while he ponders whether he will take some. He has a moral problem because his inclination is clashing with his judgment and conscience. There is here no moral dilemma in the sense in which one moral demand clashes with another. The moral resolution of his difficulty is not to yield to temptation. Such a situation is *a* common, and for children *the* common moral situation. And perhaps for adults too.

(b) Using Sartre's example, a young man has the moral obligation (based on the principle of minimization of suffering) to stay home and look after his ailing mother. As well, he has the obligation (based on the principle of freedom and justice) to resist aggression by joining the underground. He cannot do both. *Ex hypothesis* both claims weight equally. He is in a typical moral dilemma. What shall he do? From the social moral point of view it is entirely arbitrary which of these two courses of action to take. He is free to choose either one; and there is no moral praise or blame attached to either course of action. If he does one or the other, the dilemma is resolved.

(c) In a relatively affluent free society one political group advocates a public policy of redistributing wealth to the poorer members (based on the principle of fairness and equality) while another group opposes the policy on the grounds that the more wealthy deserve their wealth since they freely competed for it. This is another typical kind of dilemma where principles of justice and freedom clash. But this example differs from (b) in that here it is not necessary to do one or the other. Both moral claims can and must be recognized. Compromise is clearly indicated as a resolution to the dilemma.

In all three of the above cases moral rules and principles operated as they should have. Also in all three examples the principles led to a resolution of the moral problem. So there is every reason to acquire knowledge of the rules and principles. To rail against the fact that sometimes the application of principles leads to cruel moral dilemmas is to rail against the human condition, not against the failure of principles to do their work. What one learns in contemplating moral dilemmas is something about the human predicament, not something about morality. Moreover, the standard moral situation is *not* the dilemma at all, as in examples (b) and (c), but the temptation situation as in example (a). The standard moral outrage against theft, vandalism, discrimination, brutality, bullying, rape, violence, murder, greed, cheating on income taxes, selfishness, meanness, thoughtlessness, and so on and on cannot be accounted for nor explained in terms of competing moral claims typical of the dilemma; but they can be explained in terms of failure to have learnt and internalized moral rules and principles and/or failure of habit and will to put them into practice. In other words they are explained in terms of failure of children, and youth, and adults, to do the right thing for the right reason; failure, that is, in the achievement of virtue.

How then does one get others to do the right thing for the right reason? What methods can reliably be used? Is there any evidence to suggest what might be done? To these questions we now turn.

A Methodology for the Achievement of Virtue

What this section of the model is concerned with is presenting in sketch form three elements of a procedural or methodological nature for bringing about the achievement of virtue. In broad terms the sketch answers the question, 'How is virtue achieved?' In an attempt to keep the model simple and easy to grasp, we will use the following terms for the three elements: exemplification, encouragement, and enlightenment. The reason for referring to these as three elements of procedure rather than three separate procedures is that they are in practice ideally united into one methodology. They are here presented under separate sub-headings for discussion purposes only.

Exemplification
By the term 'exemplification' is meant the provision of ideal examples or models. The findings of scientific psychology confirm our perceptions from everyday experience that children and adolescents pattern their behaviour on others, particularly on those adults, such as parents and school teachers, who represent for the child significant persons in his environment. Richard McSweeney reports that:

> There is enough evidence to suggest that significant persons in the environment of the child and of the adolescent contribute substantially to the assimilation of values ... [A] favourable home climate of parental warmth and kindly discipline facilitates the mechanism of interiorization [of values]....[21]

Urie Brofenbrenner, as a result of his own studies and in review of others' work on modelling such as Bandura, Ross, Walters, Neal, Bryan and others, in *Two Worlds of Childhood* notes:

> It is quite clear that such qualities as mutual trust, kindness, cooperation, and social responsibility ... are learned from other human beings who in some measure exhibit these

qualities.... Or, as Walter Fenno Dearborn used to put it: 'He's a chip off the old block — not because he was knocked off it, but because he knocked around with it'.[22]

And once again Brofenbrenner says:

> One of the most salient developments in American social psychology during the past decade has been what for many laymen may appear as a demonstration of the obvious: namely, children learn by watching others.[22]

It is not necessary then to belabour the obvious. That modelling is effective is not in question. If the foregoing analysis is correct, what *should* be modelled is also not in question. How to guarantee for the child the right sort of model is more of a problem because it involves questions of jurisdiction and rights to influence a child. These questions cannot be discussed here. But one implication for teacher education can quickly be drawn. If teachers are significant models for the child, then it behoves teacher educators to admit to training institutions those who, in addition to all the other prerequisites, also have the moral requisites. (One hardly dares to elaborate on what this implies.) The other thing that can be said is that in the preparation of teachers, a broader conception of the teacher's role must be taken. As Brofenbrenner says:

> Not only must [the teacher] function as a motivating model, but it becomes her responsibility to seek out, develop, and coordinate the activities of other appropriate models and reinforcing agents both within the classroom and outside.[23]

But the element of exemplification is not the only means to get children and adolescents to do the right thing. In addition, there is the element referred to earlier as encouragement.

Encouragement

By encouragement is meant the use of techniques by the adult model to get children to follow through in behaviour as modelled. The techniques used are normally verbal praise and blame as well as non-verbal reward and punishment. (The latter is only euphemistically called encouragement; it is more accurately described as enforcement.) McSweeney observes:

> [A] degree of stability is brought about by the operation of controls, both external and internal. From outside, these sanctions, exercised by membership and reference groups,

take the form of rewards and punishments; from within, the controls arise from the development of conscience and the need for belongingness in, and acceptance by, the group.[24]

The function of moral praise and blame ('That's a good boy!' or 'That was naughty of you') is not very mysterious. They act as reminders of previous moral leanings, as on-the-spot checks of the appropriateness of responses newly elicited by modelling and teaching, and as mild and covert forms of punishment and reward. They have both a teaching and a reinforcing function.

Much more questionable is the use of overt reward and punishment for purposes of moral education. This is an area where much more social scientific research is needed. It seems to be fairly clear that reward and punishment work, that is, that people's overt behaviour can be changed in the desired direction by providing rewards and punishments, at least temporarily, and that may be one socially desirable reason for using enforcement as a last resort. But what one wants to know is if they are useful as techniques for rational moral training and education. There seems to be little reluctance to use rewards, though a great deal to use punishment; and from one perspective this seems justifiable. If the same ends can be accomplished through the use of either, then the use of rewards is preferable, because pleasure is inherently good and pain inherently evil. But from another perspective it makes little difference, since neither pain nor pleasure are adequate reasons for doing the right thing. So we will examine briefly the severer case of punishment to see if it has any potential for the achievement of virtue. Three possible justifications for its use can be entertained. The first is that through the use of punishment habits of behaviour are formed which can be of benefit as one later arrives at full moral understanding. Peter McPhail observes:

> Habit is a great (perhaps the greatest) motivational force. If we educate children in a considerate style of life, they will be considerate even to those who are not considerate to them. The habit will be very hard to break.[25]

The passage is a bit confused — habit is not a motivation — but the point about the strength of habit in difficult straits is well made. A similar point is made by A.J. Watt. Referring to Kohlberg's stages of moral development he says:

> if someone will stay with a conventional, authority-oriented approach to morality, there is every reason to do anything

possible to ensure that their authoritative conventions are in reasonable accord with the demands of rationality. Even those who are destined to progress to autonomy might find the transition smoother if it does not involve discarding large segments of the morality to which they had previously been committed.[26]

In other words, it is wise to inculcate good habits of behaviour early, even before children reach the age of reason, so we can capitalize on them later. This gives rise to what has been called the paradox of moral education which will be discussed below.

The second possible justification for use of punishment concerns the probability that children learn from it something about the relative severity of certain moral injunctions and prescriptions. A mild rebuke for bullying and a severe punishment for thoughtlessness, rather than vice versa, gives a child the wrong sense of what in the scale of things is important in morality. Appropriate punishment can lead to appropriate assessment of severity of various forms of moral turpitude.

The third consideration is less clear. It concerns the claims made by some that punishment has a morally uplifting quality. Gilbert Geis, a criminologist, has remarked that 'A period spent as an inmate in a penal facility has the wonderful power to inculcate moral virtues'.[27] John Doe, writing under a pseudonym from within a prison where he is serving a life sentence for murder, writes: 'I spent six months in solitary confinement ... grappling with questions of guilt and conscience. It was probably the most spiritually rewarding time of my life'.[28] Perhaps impressions one gets from claims like these are misleading. Perhaps not. Such claims suggest further research into limited and judicious use of punishment for their effect on moral learning.

The two methodological elements so far discussed, exemplification and encouragement, are in themselves insufficient for the achievement of virtue. Consistent with the theoretical considerations above, the fully educated person must do the right thing for the right reason. It is the provision of right reasons through the methods of enlightenment that constitutes the third, and on the view here taken, the most important, methodological element. Despite its importance there will be space only for a brief outline and comment.

Enlightenment
By enlightenment is meant the development of those cognitive ele-

ments of morality required for arriving at right reasons for action normally provided by the usual forms of verbal instruction. The areas in which enlightenment is required are: moral concepts, moral rules and principles, moral reasoning, and moral philosophy.[29]

Instruction in moral concepts   If children are to be taught to reason in morality they must have an understanding of the concepts in which they think. These concepts must be taught them. They need to understand how basic moral notions like 'good', 'right', and 'ought' function in a moral context. A useful exercise might be to get them to see the distinction between a 'good knife' and a 'good boy', reflecting Kant's hypothetical/categorical distinction. They also need a full understanding of such moral notions as theft, lying, murder, in which the moral injunctions are written into the concepts themselves, as Kovesi showed.[30] Lying, for example, is not merely uttering what is false, but deliberately deceiving for unjustified personal advantage. Untruthfulness is not necessarily lying. Other concepts such as loyalty, courage, conscientiousness (usually considered moral virtues) also need to be understood for what they are — conditional moral notions. Their moral status, if any, rests on whether they are attached to justifiable ends. (The SS was very loyal to Hitler indeed.) These few examples illustrate how complex some moral concepts are; and children, and adults too, frequently have an insufficient grasp of them. More than likely, although this needs empirical verification, children learn moral concepts most reliably by ostension, by pointing to examples of them, either in stories or in real life.

Instruction in moral rules and principles   We have already remarked on the importance of rules and principles and what they are. There is space only for one further comment regarding their nature and acquisition. To have understood a rule or principle means to have understood that instances have common characteristics which make them fall within the same class. Principles of morality cannot operate without concrete instances. So instances need to be pointed out. Everyday observations of how children learn rules suggest that someone (probably mother) repeatedly enjoined a, b and c, and regularly prohibited m, n and o. Only later, when the child grasped principles x and y of which the enjoinders and prohibitions were instances, did he understand why and was able to go on making good judgments on his own.

Instruction in moral reasoning   There is of course reasoning involved in the learning of principles. But there is further reasoning involved in the application of principles to arrive at judgments in practical cases. In the present context we refer to the latter. With respect to this, the debate in moral education is centred around the juxtaposition of 'form' with 'content' — 'form' usually referring to the way in which beliefs are regarded (authoritatively, critically, etc.) and 'content' referring to the beliefs themselves. This is a misleading way to pose the problem if what we are interested in is an analysis of how practical moral judgments are made. If there is a form or procedure for moral judgment, it is more fruitfully discussed in terms of inductive, deductive, or analogical thinking. The last refers to drawing close analogies between a prevailing moral situation and a model situation, as in the example of the Good Samaritan. It has been argued elsewhere that the moral judgment involves all three of the above.[31] With respect to deduction, for example, it must be made plain to children that the practical syllogism includes a value premise and a factual premise if a valid moral conclusion is to be drawn. The kind of instructional devices that might be used are formulating and explicating moral premises and checking for accuracy in working out the syllogism. Or one might put students into an 'intellectual jam' by getting them to agree on a conclusion arrived at intuitively and then chasing down the hidden value premise, and so on.

Instruction in moral philosophy   It has also been argued elsewhere[32] that the study of moral philosophy can contribute to sharper judgment and reasoning in morality. A rough outline of the argument is as follows: to make sound moral judgments requires sound moral reasoning and adequate grounding for reasons. This in turn requires knowledge of the nature of reasoning and knowledge of the ultimate grounds for moral principles. And if it is philosophy's task to analyze the reasoning and explicate the ultimate ground for principles, then philosophy can have the effect of improving judgment in practical situations. There is some evidence that this is the case, although it is far from conclusive. This is another area for further empirical investigation.

Brief though the sketch of the role of enlightenment has been, it is this methodological element that advances this model over the so-called traditional methods of moral education, in which modelling and the use of sanctions together with plenty of instruction in, but no examination of, conventional rules constituted the primary method of rearing children. The employment of the three elements — exemplification, encouragement, and enlightenment — resembles well-worn and well-known practices. Indeed the typical case of informal moral learning is an adult, say a parent, modelling good behaviour before the youngster, eliciting from the youngster the appropriate response. The response is monitored on the spot followed by praise or blame, and even punishment, when nothing else works. Ideally reasons and explanations go hand in hand with the sanctions. That is why it was noted earlier that the three elements are really one methodology. Obviously in formal situations, such as in schools, a good deal of instruction for enlightenment can fruitfully be done separately, with use of imagined or artificial cases. Even this is quite traditional. But the insistence in this model on right reason is what marks its departure from tradition. The radical difference is that the behaviour to be modelled, the rules taught, and reasons given, are justified on rational moral grounds and seen by the child so to be justified and for the child himself able eventually so to justify them. And when justification is pressed home to fundamental principles, tradition may be upset; practices may change; social instability may ensure. The habit of using reason may challenge and change religious, political, and legal practices. If reason is king, then when the force of reason confronts the power of tradition, tradition must yield. So what looks like a very traditional model can, when effective moral enlightenment properly forms part of it, turn out to be a major force in changing traditions for the better. It is in any case spurious to argue that the model is deficient because it resembles traditional child-rearing methods. What matters is the cogency of the arguments and the empirical reliability of the factual claims.

The question of empirical reliability takes us back to where we began when we noted that Kohlberg's theory of moral development, despite its weaknesses, continues to be used as a research model because apparently no other model is available. If the model presented here in thumb-nail sketch is acceptable, then it is no longer necessary to rely on Kohlberg's model. And there are key differences. This model enlarges the scope of empirical investigation to include the significant process of what has been called exemplification and encouragement. Indeed, as we saw, much research has been conducted in these areas and much more needs to be done. But in the area of moral reasoning there also is a departure from Kohlberg. On this model it is not the *form* of moral reasoning, or the attitude toward moral reasoning, that is assessed as a function of social interaction and cognitive stimulation, as in Kohlberg, but the *con-*

tent, the reasons themselves, that are philosophically assessed as reasonably derivative from moral principles, such reasoning also empirically assessed as functions of direct instruction in rules and principles. The assessment of reasons is not a matter for empirical investigation; the ability to assess them as a function of instruction is, and can and probably should be done.[33] But one suspects that the results of such investigation would, as in Brofenbrenner's investigation into modelling, confirm the obvious. For here, as so often in education, once we know precisely what it is we want to achieve, the method to do so readily becomes apparent. In moral education the major questions still are 'What is virtue?' and 'What are the virtues?', not 'How is virtue taught?' For the latter, as Gilbert Ryle has observed,[34] we need to reflect on familiar experiences from the classroom and the crèche. For the former we may have to turn a more acute ear to moral philosophy.

The Paradox of Moral Education

Moral education, considered in the light of the full implication of the concept 'education', requires reasoned understanding of the moral rules and principles voluntarily accepted for oneself. But before children reach the age of reason, they must act and behave on the basis of less than understanding of these principles. Necessarily habits of behaviour are formed early in life. Because it is thought that habitual behaviour militates against reasoned behaviour there is in moral education, as well as in other areas of education, a paradox; the pedagogy employed seems to be at odds with the ideals aimed at. This phenomenon has led to the production of a volume of literature, beginning with Aristotle, on the paradox of moral education. One way of thinking about the paradox and its solution is to articulate it in terms of temporal and logical sequencing. The temporal order of moral learning, or the sequence according to which children achieve moral understanding, can be depicted as follows:

1 Habituation in moral practice (truth-telling, being kind, etc.). e.g., Habitually lining up at the playground slide.
2 Making judgments in particular cases with respect to moral practice (learning the concept and applying it in real cases). e.g., I ought not to jump the queue.
3 Justifying the judgment on the basis of a particular moral rule. e.g., Jumping queues is not fair.
4 Justifying the rule on the basis of a moral principle.

e.g., Not being fair is a violation of (offence against) justice because it arbitrarily makes one an exception without a real relevant difference.

5 Justifying moral principles in a way of life.

e.g., No exception without relevant differences is the mark of a rational person and is presupposed in a rational way of life. The moral way of life improves the human condition.

The logical order, that is, the order that would be ideal in some purely non-realistic, non-human rational world, would be the exact reverse of the above. The movement would be from (5) to (1). The opposite directions of the logical order and the temporal order lead to the apparent contradiction and the paradox. There is, however, no real contradiction here; there is only a pedagogical problem that is best solved by ensuring that the low-level rules children learn, and the habits they form on the basis of them, are actually reasonable moral rules and habits. If that is so, then habit will not militate against reason; and one can confidently teach low-level content without fear of charges of illegitimate conditioning and indoctrination. Moral education can then be genuinely so called.

Suggested further readings:

HAMM, C.M. (1985) 'Moral education as the achievement of virtue' in *Melbourne Studies in Education*, pp. 225–44.

HAMM, C.M. (1977) 'The content of moral education, or in defence of the "Bag of Virtues"', in *The School Review*, February, pp. 218–28.

HERSH, R., MILLER, J. and FIELDING, G. (1980) *Models of Moral Education*, New York, Longman,

KAZEPIDES, A.C. (1977) 'The logic of values clarification' in *The Journal of Educational Thought*, 11, 2, pp. 99–111.

PETERS, R.S. (1963) 'Reason and habit: The paradox of moral education' in NIBLETT W.R. (Ed.) *Moral Education in a Changing Society*, London, Faber & Faber, pp. 46–65. (Also in SCHEFFLER, I. (1966) (Ed.) *Philosophy of Education* (2nd Edition), Allyn and Bacon.)

PETERS, R.S. (1979) 'Form and content in moral education' in COCHRANE, D.B., HAMM, C.M. and KAZEPIDES, A.C. (Eds.) *The Domain of Moral Education*, Paulist Press and O.I.S.E., pp. 187–202.

Notes

1 See HAMM, C.M. and DANIELS, L.B. (1979) 'Moral education in relation to values education' in COCHRANE, D.B., HAMM, C.M. and

KAZEPIDES, A.C. (Eds.) *The Domain of Moral Education*, Paulist Press and OISE, pp. 17–34.

2 For such an argument see HAMM, C. (1986) 'Moral education and the distinction between social and personal morality' in *Westminster Studies in Education*, 8, pp. 37–58.

3 See for example: GOW K. (1980) *Yes Virginia, There is Right and Wrong*, Toronto, Wiley, and HERSH R., MILLER J. AND FIELDING G. (1980) *Models of Moral Education* New York, Longman.

4 For a good summary statement of Kohlberg's thesis see CARTER R.E., (1984) *Dimensions of Moral Education*, Toronto, University of Toronto Press, pp. 203–6.

5 NICOLAYEV J. and PHILLIPS D.C. (1979) 'On assessing Kohlberg's stage theory of moral development,' in Cochrane D.B. HAMM, C.M. and KAZEPIDES, A.C. (Eds.), *op. cit*, p. 247.

6 *Ibid.*, pp. 248–9.

7 For a full description of the main ideas of values clarification see RATHS, L. *et al.* (1966) *Values and Teaching*, Charles E. Merrill Books, Inc.

8 HAMM, C. (1985) 'Moral education and the distinction between social and personal morality', in *Westminster Studies in Education*, 8, pp. 37–58.

9 PETERS, R.S. (1966) *Ethics and Education*, London, George Allen and Unwin, p. 31.

10 LORING, L.M. (1966) *Two Kinds of Value*, London, Routledge and Kegan Paul, p.19.

11 WARNOCK, G.J. (1970) *The Object of Morality*, London, Methuen, p. 16.

12 PETERS R.S. *Ethics and Education, op. cit., passim.*

13 *Ibid*, p. 114.

14 *Ibid*, p. 115.

15 FRANKENA W., (1966) 'Toward a philosophy of moral education,' in SCHEFFLER I. (Ed.) *Philosophy and Education*, 2nd ed., Boston, Allyn and Bacon, p. 225ff.

16 *The Ethics Of Aristotle*, trans. J.A.K. Thomson, London, Allen and Unwin, 1953, pp. 55–6.

17 KOHLBERG, L. (1970) 'Education for justice: A modern statement of the Platonic views', in SIZER, N.F. and SIZER, J.R. (Eds.), *Moral Education: Five Lectures*, Cambridge, Mass., Harvard University Press.

18 WILSON, J. (1979) 'Moral components and moral education,' in Cochrane, Hamm and Kazepides, *op. cit.*, p. 181.

19 TELFER, E. (1980) *Happiness* London, Macmillan, p. 128.

20 MILNE, R.A. (1984) 'Moral development in early childhood', Ph.D. thesis, University of Melbourne, p. 197.

21 McSWEENEY, R. (1972) 'A socio-psychological approach to an understanding of the value concept', in *Values: Education and Society*, Mercy College Institute of Social Order Publication, pp. 17–8.

22 BROFENBRENNER, U. (1970) *Two Worlds of Childhood: US and USSR* New York, Russell Sage Foundation, p. 117.

22 *Ibid.*, p. 124.
23 *Ibid.*, p. 154.
24 McSweeney, R. (1972) *op. cit.*, p. 17.
25 McPhail, P. (1982) *Social and Moral Education*, Oxford, Basil Black-well, p. 121.
26 Watt, A.J. (1976) *Rational Moral Education*, Melbourne University Press, pp. 55–6.
27 *Vancouver Sun*, 1 November 1971.
28 *Ibid.*, 22 January 1980.
29 See Hamm C. (1990) 'The logic of moral instruction: An analysis of the cognitive content of morality, and the implication of this analysis for moral education', Ph.D. thesis, University of London.
30 Kovesi J., (1967) *Moral Notions*, London, Routledge and Kegan Paul.
31 Hamm, C. (1970) . . ., *op. cit.*, Chapter 6.
32 Hamm, C. (1978) 'The study of ethics as moral education', in *The Journal of Educational Thought* 12, August, pp. 115–30.
33 Such research has in fact already begun. See for example Haines, A.T. Jackson, M.S. and Davidson, J. 'Children's resistance to the temptation to steal in real and hypothetical situations: A comparison of two treatment programs,' *Australian Psychologist*, 18, 3, November 1983, pp. 289–303. The authors report that a form of 'direct instruction' produced 'significantly better resistance behaviour in hypothetical temptation to steal situations' than did a 'general instructional program' based on Kohlberg's model for moral development courses.
34 Ryle, G. (1972) 'Can virtue be taught?', in Dearden, R.F., Hirst, P.H. and Peter, R.S. (Eds.), *Education and the Development of Reason*, London, Routledge and Kegan Paul, pp. 434–47.

Questions and Exercises

Answer each of the following questions in a few sentences:

1 In what sense is the term 'values education' redundant?
2 What is the point and purpose of moral discourse?
3 What are some major weaknesses in Kohlberg's theory of moral education?
4 What are some major weaknesses in 'values clarification' as a method of moral education?
5 Does successful socialization guarantee moral education? Explain.
6 If morality is 'doing the right thing for the right reason', what constitutes 'right reason'? Can right reasons be taught to children?
7 'It is better to do the right thing for the wrong reason or no reason, than not doing the right thing at all'. Explain.
8 What are the problems of relying nearly exclusively on the moral dilemma in discussions engaged in for purposes of moral education?
9 Why is modelling so important for purposes of moral education?
10 Why is formation of good habits very important in early moral education/training programmes?

11   In what areas of concern can instruction in morality reasonably occur?
12   What is the paradox of moral education? Why is it a paradox?
13   Does relativity in local moral rules mean that morality is necessarily non-objective at a moral fundamental level and hence entirely arbitrary? Explain.
14   Is the state (public) school value neutral? Could it ever be? Explain.
15   What does it mean to say that morality is overriding? Provide some examples.
16   Does the fact that sometimes there are moral dilemmas mean that moral reasoning and moral judgment is arbitrary? Explain.

Write a short essay (not more than 500 words) on each of the following:
1   On what basis can one distinguish between various kinds of values? Provide examples of the various kinds you distinguish. Are there various types of justification for each kind? Explain.
2   Can religious education serve as a substitute for (or be equivalent to) moral education? In your discussion specify precisely what you mean by 'religious education' and 'moral education'.
3   What specifically would you teach if you were given a block of time in regular school hours to provide moral education? Justify your choice of content.
4   Name and briefly describe the fundamental moral principles (not derived rules and principles necessary for rational moral discourse to occur. Are the principles you cite both necessary and sufficient for the foundation of morality?
5   What are some major objectives to the teaching of content in a moral education program? Can these objectives be met? If so, how?

CHAPTER 10

The Justification of Education

The Nature of the Justification

To provide a justification for a course of action is to provide good reasons or grounds for that course of action. It is to show by argument the rightness of that action. To suggest that education must be justified is to suggest that the public school, if it is to be an educational institution, cannot simply be satisfied to take on roles at random in reaction to public pressures or traditional roles based on authority, on speculations about human nature, or on untestable metaphysical assumptions. Judgment about what is worthwhile to pass on the children requires reasoned argument. This chapter will attempt to provide such an argument.

Before we proceed it is worth reminding ourselves just exactly what it is we are making an argument for. Throughout this book, and particularly in Chapter 4, we have made the assumption that the *primary* purpose of the school is education, leaving room for peripheral roles of the school. We now want to provide further grounds for that assumption by showing why education has that importance. It should be noted that many theorists and philosophers and curriculum builders subscribe to the value of education; but often they deem it merely one value amongst many and perhaps not the most central for the schools. The difference between those theorists and the position taken here is that here the value of education is seen to be supreme. Not only is it considered of primary importance, but so overwhelmingly important that without it there would be little reason remaining for the school to exist.

But we need to be much more precise in what it is we are justifying. It will be recalled that education is the deliberate initiation into those worthwhile activities characterized by knowledge and understanding in breadth and depth. The breadth and depth requirement means that the educated person will have mastered all the extant 'forms' of knowledge and understanding available to him. The content of education that is offered to fulfill this requirement will consist of subjects such as arithmetic and geometry, nature study and chemistry, social studies and history, literature and music, psychology and philosophy, and so on, these representing various approaches to the stated forms: physical (empirical) science, pure mathematics and logic, the social 'sciences,' aesthetics, ethics, and philosophy. These six, it has been argued, constitute all extant forms of knowledge. Knowledge about religions would fall within the sphere of history.

The courses selected to introduce these 'forms' to *all* children would include the key ideas and concepts in each form and the main up-to-date findings in each of them, as well as thorough familiarization with the mode of operation in each of the disciplines. Children would come to know, for example, how historians and scientists work and discover new truths. It is envisaged that such studies would be systematic, arduous, and formal. Education implies understanding and the capacity to reason and justify beliefs and conduct; it is not merely the acquisition of skill and habit. Education is not narrow specialization, but connotes 'cognitive perspective' in which multiple experiences are connected to form coherence and consistency. What is not being argued here is a particular type of course structure and a method of teaching, nor a sequence of content presentation relative to age and experience. These are important further matters for curriculum specialists to consider. A course in automechanics is not automatically ruled out. From an educational perspective, studies about automobiles would include mathematical and chemical information; the history of the automobile; the aesthetics of form and design; their potentiality for good or ill; the role of the car in problems of pollution and town planning. Also not being argued is the superiority of one form of knowledge over another. No justification will be provided to show that biology or history, say, are more important than art or philosophy. What will be attempted will be to provide a general ethical argument for why some pursuits such as poetry and physics are more worthwhile than others such as chess and golf and why the former but not the latter are justifiably pursued in education.

Kinds of Justification

It has already been indicated that tradition, authority, and metaphysics will not do as justifications. Three other kinds of arguments will be used as constituting justifications of the appropriate kind. The first is moral in nature. If it can be shown that certain sorts of pursuits we compel children to undertake are not justified on moral grounds, that would be a very good reason to limit compulsion to a few pursuits that are justified. The second sort of justification is an instrumental one. If education is seen as a means to some other justifiable ends, then the means themselves are considered justifiable. This is not the argument that the end always justifies the means, but only that sometimes it can. Nor does an instrumental justification rule out a non-instrumental justification as well. Music could be pursued as a means to a good job as a musician and at the same time pursued as something worthwhile for its own sake. If it is the latter, then we can say the activity is worthwhile because it is intrinsically justified. Many things we do, and ultimately the most important things we do, we do for the intrinsic value in them. These sorts of things can range from climbing mountains to going to concerts, from gardening to writing poetry. We will argue below that the strongest argument for the pursuit of education is of this kind.

A Moral Argument

Some form of paternalism or maternalism in the rearing of human beings is inevitable, carrying with it the necessity to decide for the young and, most likely, to compel the young. Since on moral ground the minimum amount of compulsion is desirable, it behooves adults to choose very carefully what kind of experiences they provide for the young. The kind of experiences that qualify must meet at least two conditions:

1 they must be of the sort that children themselves would choose if they were knowledgeable adults; and
2 they must be the kind of experiences that they would likely not have unless they were compelled to have them.

This would seem to rule out of educational curricula such activities as games, physical exercise, narrow skill training, vocational trades, and otherwise easily acquired information and understanding. These types of learning can easily be 'picked up' without compulsion and are not considered central to the child's own long-term well-being. An argument similar to this was considered earlier in Chapter 6. All this argument achieves, however, is to rule out a few things that cannot be justified as educational; it does not indicate why education as construed above is worthy of pursuit. A more promising start than that is to consider an instrumental argument.

Instrumental Justification

One of the most common types of justification for the pursuit of education is its instrumental value. Children want to know what the 'use' of education is; and politicians want to know what good it will do in society and for the economy. That education, conceived of as knowledge in breadth and depth, is useful for the receiver of it as well as beneficial for the community as a whole cannot be denied. It would be very surprising if a person with education could not do something and be something better than he would without it and so benefit both himself and his community.

One successful argument for the pursuit of education pertains to the depth of understanding required for education. Depth of understanding in such areas as chemistry, mathematics, physics, art, and logic may lead to specialized trainings in nutrition, medicine, engineering, communications and so on, all of which are amenities of contemporary communal life. Knowledge, rather than mere beliefs or opinions, is necessary for predictability and control over the natural order as well as the social order.

An equally successful argument for the pursuit of education pertains to the breadth of understanding required for education. Various occupations require breadth of understanding on the job. Not only is flexibility required for successful performance on the job, but rapid changes in technology and social changes require corresponding retraining and adjustment to new situations. Those who have the widest possible understanding of a job also have the best chances of promotion to positions of responsibility. Breadth of understanding renders possible a much more intelligent choice of occupation that one can satisfactorily and happily undertake in the first place. There is, too, the argument that breadth of understanding is ideal preparation for democratic participation in a community. Human institutions are more humane and effective as a result of people understanding each other and the various roles people play in a civilized community.

The above are just a few of the very obvious benefits accruing to an individual and a community as a result of education. A justification for education in terms of such utilities is, however, difficult to sustain. There is some force to such instrumental argument; but it does not take us very far. First, it must be remembered that benefits referred to are, as it were, by-products, of education. Education is something we pursue because it is valuable in its own right; and we would pursue it even if the by-products were not there. The primary justification, in other words, seems to lie elsewhere, despite the secondary justification of utility. Furthermore, it might be that the benefits alluded to would accrue even if our primary goal was other than education, say, the goal of job training, democratic citizenship training, or public relations. Just because education produces some desirable benefits, it might still be the case that the same benefits are obtainable by means other than purely education. Finally, and more fundamentally, the instrumentalist argument is unsatisfactory and incomplete because the ends for which the mentioned utilities are the means are themselves left unjustified, and it would be a mad and meaningless chase if all activities were merely means to something else and no judgment were ever passed on the end-state or the intrinsic, non-instrumental value placed on human activities. To justify education is in the end to justify a way of life pursued for its own sake; it is to justify the good life itself. Those who seek to justify the good life in terms of pleasure and happiness argue that educational activities are precisely those that provide the conditions for the achievement of that pleasure and happiness.

The Pleasure Principle as Justification

Those who hold to a utilitarian view of ethics also hold to a utilitarian view of education. They argue that education is justified to the extent that it provides on balance long-term benefit and happiness, such happiness interpreted in terms of pleasure satisfaction. Pleasure, then, is the end to which all human activity, including education, is the means. There is something attractive about such an argument. Finding enjoyment and pleasure is certainly one of the foremost reasons why people do things. It would be very surprising if the good life had nothing to do with pleasure and enjoyment and if education never provided such enjoyment.

There are, however, a number of reasons why an account of the worthwhile in terms of pleasure is unsatisfactory. First, the activities we pursue in education, say, a sustained effort in solving an algebraic problem, are sometimes void of pleasure. There is certainly satisfaction in solving the problem but that can hardly be termed 'pleasure'. Of course, the term 'pleasure' can be used in such a way that it covers all cases of human motivation and so make it true by definition that all things are ultimately done for pleasure. That indeed is the problem with a theory known as psychological hedonism. If, however, one wants to make a factual observation about why people do things and assert that it is pleasure, then the claim is hard to sustain. Can a gruelling mountain-climbing expedition be said to be a pleasure? Perhaps in response to, 'Why did they do it?' the answer forthcoming might be, 'For the pleasure that's in it!' But that expression used in that context, as R.S. Peters has correctly observed, means 'done for its own sake'.[1] It serves to deny that the action was done instrumentally. It does not mean that the mountaineers actually had sensations of pleasure. And this joins on to another reason why the pleasure principle cannot function as a justification. The nature of the satisfaction involved in the activity cannot be described apart from mentioning the activity itself. The distinction between means and ends collapses in these cases. So the justification for pursuit of the activity lies in the activity itself, not in some extrinsic value such as pleasure which the activity serves. The value is in the activity. We do not, for example, first discover that there is pleasure in helping someone in need and then decide it is a morally worthwhile thing to do. We first decide on the moral appropriateness of helping and only then, if at all, find pleasure in doing so. And that pleasure can only be described as the pleasure of helping someone in need. So once again we see that pleasure is not the justification for the moral action and for moral education. Still another reason pleasure is inadequate as a justification, also mentioned by Peters, is that some pleasurable things are trivial. Not only are some worthwhile things not pleasurable, but some pleasurable things are not worthwhile. Peters mentions such things as sun-bathing and eating opium. The point is that judgments are made on the things we want and those judgments are not made in terms of the pleasure involved, or certainly not always and centrally, as utilitarians claim. In the justification of education, pleasure cannot be the characterization of the worthwhile things that constitute the reasons for pursuing them.

Non-Instrumental (Intrinsic) Justification

What is there, then, that educational activities have in virtue of which it can be said that they are worthwhile? Peters argues that there is something about educational curricular activities themselves which constitute reasons for pursuing them. There is something about the character of knowledge and understanding that in itself counts as justification. According to Peters, whose argument we shall now follow, there are two types of value in knowledge and understanding that provide the grounds:

1 those related to the absence of boredom and intellectual absorption; and
2 those values implicit in the demands of reason.

Values Related to Intellectual Absorption

The knowledge and understanding required for education provides opportunity for the exercise of intellectual skill and competence. Such mental activity is both fascinating and absorbing; hence Peters calls it a value related to the absence of boredom. As educated people, we invent rules and conventions and superimpose them on our activities so we can present ourselves with challenges and fascinations otherwise impossible. Even on activities that are clearly pleasurable in themselves, we set up elaborate conventions to engage the mind; so instead of merely eating or having sex, we dine and make love. Educational activities provide the occasion for the exercise of these sorts of intellectual skills.

Educational activities also afford opportunity for planning and ordering our lives. Much knowledge and information, particularly historical and sociological information about how people live and work and shape their lives, will enable us to avoid unnecessary conflict in life and enable us to harmonize our life goals. It will help us set our priorities amongst golf, gardening, and girls or between bread-baking and boys. Aristotle thought the essential ingredient for happiness was integration of life. Here education plays a vital role.

The activities engaged in while pursuing education provide opportunity for duration of the escape from boredom. The goods of education are, in other words, permanent and limitless. Unlike food and sex and material goods, educational goods survive and increase over time. There is no limit to the pursuit of truth; the more of it we share, the more there is. In education there is possibility for unlimited development and growth with permanent satisfaction. It is no wonder that Plato once remarked that the keenest pleasures are the pleasures of the mind.

But even these considerations are insufficient for the justification of education. The argument is still very much of a naturalistic and instrumental kind. Some people just do not find the kind of pleasure in education that Peters refers to. Even if they do, the pursuit of more down-to-earth pleasures rates for them fairly highly alongside education. Furthermore, much of the above argument about the value of education as a method to escape boredom could apply also to non-educational activities such as chess and other games. Indeed some of the criticism levied against Peters is in error because the critics have not progressed further in Peters' argument than to this stage. P.S. Wilson, for example, argues that since one must know about bingo before one is able to play it and because bingo offers a source of enjoyment, it (bingo) is, as far as Peters' argument is concerned, just as valuable as education.[2] Wilson is mistaken, however, because he does not take into account the next stage in Peters' argument to show why poetry is more important than Bingo and other games.

Values Related to the Demands of Reason

Educational activities differ from games in that they are concerned with knowledge and truth; and the benefits of knowledge and truth are *not merely* those of providing escape from boredom. In fact sometimes the search for truth is just a lot of hard work and it would be difficult to establish, even with a careful calculus in long terms, that in the end the truth provided a pay-off in pleasure. But to the educated person that does not matter. To him truth matters supremely, even if the effort to free the mind of prejudice and error is toilsome and frustrating. As a truth-seeker he acquires habits of truth-telling, of seriousness and sincerity, of non-arbitrariness and impartiality, of consistency and a sense of relevance, of respect for evidence and respect for people as sources of evidence.

But why is it that truth-seeking is for the educated *qua* educated persons the most worthwhile human activity? It is not merely because truth is a source of pleasure, which it can indeed also be, but because truth is presupposed in any attempt to live a life of reason and in any attempt to justify (give reasons for) a way of life. If one asks, 'What ought I to do?' or 'Why do this rather than that?'

one presupposes, is already committed to, a life of reason and to truth-seeking. Peters says:

> If a justification is sought for doing X rather than Y, then firstly X and Y have to be distinguished in some way. To distinguish them we have to rely on the forms of discrimination which are available, to locate them within some kind of conceptual scheme.... So an open-ended employment of various forms of understanding is necessary. And such probing must be conducted at least on the presupposition that obvious misconceptions of what is involved in these activities is to be removed. There is a presumption, in other words, that it is undesirable to believe what is false and desirable to believe what is true.[3]

The possession of knowledge and understanding in many forms can be shown to be valuable in themselves because they are necessarily presupposed in the working out of the valuing mind. Further, no one in a civilized state of mind can escape the kind of valuing about how to live one's life. Therefore no one can escape the call for reason and truth. Peters, in the same article, goes on to say:

> Man is thus a creature who lives under the demands of reason.... How does it help the argument to show that human life is only intelligible on the assumption that the demands of reason are admitted, and woven into the fabric of human life? It helps because it makes plain that the demands of reason are not just an option available to the reflective.... (H)uman life ... bears witness to the demands of reason. Without acceptance by men of such demands their life would be unintelligible.... Concern for truth is written into human life.[4]

Education then is the answer to the demands of reason in life. There are those who are ready to admit that education is valuable and that it consists in knowledge and understanding who nevertheless wish to deny its importance because it requires so much time and effort. They, in parody of Falstaff, say, 'If that be education; I'll have none of it'. But we see now why they, like Falstaff, cannot escape the demands of living a fully human life. To have participated in civilized life is to have entered the fray. Education not only answers to the demands for reason but sets the demands for reason. It not only enables one to answer but also to ask, 'Why do this rather than that?' We do not first have a demand for reason in life and then find that education helps us to satisfy this demand. Rather, as we become educated we find the demands of reason increasing as our capacity to understand increases. Not to have understood and not to have given room to the demands of reason, is not to have lived a worthwhile life at all. As Peters says, 'Education, properly understood, is the attempt to actualize the ideal implicit in Socrates' saying that the unexamined life is not worth living'.[5]

If education, then, essentially amounts to the acquisition of knowledge and understanding for purposes of examining life, could one not argue that such an examination of life is too troublesome and not worth the effort? Well, hardly. One who argues that the examined life is not worth living, places himself in a very awkward position. Anyone who attempts consistently to argue that the rational life of education is not worth living, and tries to give reasons why we should not be concerned with truth and knowledge, is already engaged in the rational life and exhibits concern for truth and knowledge. Such a person relies on a denial of his own premise. Only one who has examined, or is still examining life, is in a position to argue that the unexamined life is worth living; but that cannot consistently be argued. It is logically impossible cogently and consistently to argue against the value of education, for education is required so to argue. It is, however, logically possible to refuse to get an education or to have as little to do with it as possible; but such people have cut themselves off from rational argument, from participation in the discussion about how to live wisely, even from coherent thought and speech itself. They have no argument; no rights; no voice. All they can consistently do is remain silent.

The above argument, known as the transcendental argument (or the transcendental deduction) for the justification of education was first published by Peters in *Ethics and Education*, Chapter 5, under the title 'Worthwhile activities'. A revised and further developed form of the argument appeared under the title, 'The justification of education' in 1973. Since the publication of these two papers there has been a barrage of criticism regarding that argument, though the criticism has been largely ineffective in destroying the argument. The view taken here is that the argument is fundamentally sound; but that it is insufficient in completely depicting what constitutes the good life and the good for man which education strives to achieve. While it is true that we cannot escape from the demands of reason if we wish to participate in a civilized form of social life and so must become broadly interested truth-seekers and committed to education, it is also true that we cannot escape from our non-rational animal nature and those deep-seated desires and proclivities that we are either born with or develop early in life which constitute part of our make-up. To satisfy those desires is also part of the good life. So there is at the same time a public, objective, social demand for reason and knowledge and truth as well as a private, subjective personal demand for self-expression and fulfillment of natural desires. Utilitarians made the mistake of trying to justify the pursuit of knowledge and understanding (in a word, education) in terms of the pleasure principle. They thought they could demonstrate that unless education contributed to satisfaction of some sort of pleasure, it was not worthwhile. Not so, argued Peters. There are many pleasures that are not worthwhile and some worthwhile activities are not in any specific way pleasure-producing. But Peters very likely erred in the opposite direction by arguing that the good life is the life of reason. Because man lives under the demands of reason, satisfaction of the demands of reason through education will yield the predominant satisfactions characteristic of the good life. Peters specifically denies that education is the only desirable human undertaking. In the opening of 'The justification of education' he says that education 'obviously does not encompass all that is desirable'.[6] But he nevertheless leaves the impression that the good life is *primarily* the life of reason and that the greatest good is in developing our rational capacity maximally. But, as Crittenden has correctly observed 'We cannot simply claim that because it (education) is of such worth, it is something that everyone ought to achieve as fully as possible'.[7] This is because there are dimensions of the good life that knowledge and understanding do not satisfy. And if, as is usually agreed upon, education is concerned with those activities worthwhile in themselves characteristic of the good life, then the kind of knowledge and understanding required for education may be less theoretical and more practical and personal than it seems Peters would allow.

A position, similar to the one being hinted at here, is J. White's, in which he seeks a justification for education based on the demands of nature as well as the demands of reason.[8] This is not the occasion for an examination of his 'post-reflective desire-satisfaction' theory of education, but merely to make reference to the possibility of a more complex and compromising position that can be entertained as a reasonable alternative to utilitarianism on the one hand and Peters' transcendental deduction on the other. White's book also is a good example of the ongoing debate concerning the good life, the nature and justification of education, and the type of issue and style of debate occurring in contemporary philosophy of education.

Suggested further readings:

HIRST, P.H. and PETERS, R.S. (1970) 'Educational institutions', *The Logic of Education*, London, Routledge and Kegan Paul, pp. 106–113; 130–131.

PETERS, R.S. (1973) 'The justification of education' in PETERS R.S. (Ed.) *The Philosophy of Education*, Oxford University Press, pp. 239–267.

PETERS, R.S. (1966) 'Worthwhile activities', in *Ethics and Education*, London Routledge and Kegan Paul.

WHITE, J. (1982) *The Aims of Education Revisited*, London, Routledge and Kegan Paul, chapters 2, 3, and 6.

Notes

1 See PETERS, R.S. *Ethics and Education, op. cit.*, chapter 5.
2 See WILSON, P.S. (1967) 'In defence of bingo' in *British Journal of Educational Studies*, 15, February.
3 PETERS, R.S. (1973) 'The justification of education' in PETERS, R.S. (Ed.), *The Philosophy of Education*, Oxford University Press, p. 252.
4 *Ibid.*, p. 254, 255.
5 *Ibid.*, p. 262.
6 *Ibid.*, p. 237.
7 CRITTENDEN, B. (1973) *Education and the Social Ideal*, Longman Canada Ltd., p. 22.
8 See WHITE, J.P. (1982) *The Aims of Education Restated*, London, Routledge and Kegan Paul.

Questions and Exercises

Answer the following questions as briefly as possible:
1 Distinguish between instrumental and non-instrumental justification for education. Give examples of each.
2 R.S. Peters claims that there is a logical relation between means and ends in education. Explain, with some examples, what this means.
3 It has been claimed that the educated person is less likely to find life boring. Is that true? Do you think that that is a convincing reason to pursue education?
4 What instrumental reasons can be given for valuing knowledge and understanding in terms of social benefit?
5 Why is it unsatisfactory to give an account of the worthwhileness of education in terms of pleasure?
6 Is the uneducated life worth living? If so, would the uneducated be able to prove it?

Write a short essay in answer to the following two questions:
1 Suppose it came about that there no longer existed the need (nor possibility) for employment. Would there then be any point or purpose

in pursuing an education? If so, what would it be? If not, explain why not.

2 How would you justify the inclusion of poetry, science, and history (and the like) but not chess, bridge, or sports (and the like) in an educational curriculum? Or would you so judge? If not, why not? And on what grounds would you make your selection?

Bibliography

Note: These bibliographic entries extend beyond cited works in the text. Works not cited in the text are nevertheless relevant to the writing of the book because they informed the author's thinking either by way of concurrence or by taking views widely different and thus helped focus on the points of view expressed. Readers of the text are especially encouraged to seek alternative points of view included in these bibliographic entries in the spirit of open-mindedness and unbiased reflection.

ARCHAMBAULT, R.D. (Ed.) (1965) *Philosophical Analysis and Education*, New York, Humanities Press.

ARISTOTLE. *Nichomachean Ethics*, (any edition).

AYER, A.J. (1956) *The Problem of Knowledge*, Hammondsworth, Middlesex, Penguin Books.

BARROW, R. (1976) *Common Sense and the Curriculum*, London, Allen and Unwin.

BARROW, R. (1978) *Radical Education*, Oxford, Martin Robertson.

BARROW, R. (1981) *The Philosophy of Schooling*, Brighton, Wheatsheaf.

BARROW, R. and WOODS, R. (1988) *An Introduction to Philosophy of Education*, (3rd Edition), London, Routledge.

BENN, S.I. and PETERS, R.S. (1959) *Social Principles and the Democratic State*, London, Allen and Unwin.

BERLIN, I. (1969) *Four Essays on Liberty*, London, Oxford University Press.

BIGGE, M.L. (1982) *Educational Philosophies for Teachers*, Columbus, Ohio, Charles E. Merrill Publishing Company.

BROFENBRENNER, U. (1970) *Two Worlds of Childhood*, New York, Russell Sage Foundation.

BROUDY, H.S. (1988) *The Uses of Schooling*, New York, Routledge.

CARTER, R.E. (1984) *Dimensions of Moral Education*, Toronto, University of Toronto Press.

CHAMBERS, J. (1983) *The Achievement of Education*, New York, Harper and Row.

CHAZAN, B. and SOLTIS, F. (Eds.) (1975) *Moral Education*, New York, Teachers College Press.

CHAZAN B. (1985) *Contemporary Approaches to Moral Education*, New York, Teachers College Press.

COCHRANE, D., HAMM, C.M. and KAZEPIDES, A.C. (Eds.) (1979) *The Domain of Moral Education*, New York and Toronto, Paulist Press and Ontario Institute for Studies in Education.

COCHRANE, D. and Schiralli, M. (Eds.) (1982) *Philosophy of Education: Canadian Perspectives*, Don Mills, Ontario, Collier Macmillan Canada.

COOPER, D. (1980) *Illusions of Equality*, London, Routledge and Kegan Paul.

COOPER, D. (Ed.) (1986) *Education, Values and Mind*, London, Routledge and Kegan Paul.

CRITTENDEN, B. (1973) *Education and Social Ideals*, Don Mills, Ontario: Longman Canada Limited.

DEARDEN, R.F. (1968) *The Philosophy of Primary Education*, London, Routledge and Kegan Paul.

DEARDEN, R.F. (1984) *Theory and Practice in Education*, London, Routledge and Kegan Paul.

DEARDEN, R.F., HIRST, P.H., and PETERS, R.S. (Eds.) (1972) *Education and the Development of Reason*. London: Routledge and Kegan Paul.

DEWEY, J. (1916) *Democracy and Education*, New York, Macmillan Co.

DOWNIE, R.S. and TELFER, E. (1969) *Respect for Persons*, London, George Allen and Unwin.

DOYLE, J.F. (Ed.) (1973) *Educational Judgments*, London, Routledge and Kegan Paul.

EGAN, K. (1983) *Education and Psychology: Plato, Piaget and Scientific Psychology*, New York, Teachers College Press.

EGAN, K. and NADANER, D. (Eds.) (1988) *Imagination and Education*, New York, Teachers College Press.

ELIOT, J.S. (1962) *Notes Towards the Definition of Culture*, London, Faber.

ENTWISTLE, H. (1970) *Child-Centered Education*, London, Methuen.

FEINBERG, W. and SOLTIS, J.F. (1986) *School and Society*, New York, Teachers College Press.

FENSTERMACHER, G. and SOLTIS, J.F. (1986) *Approaches to Teaching*, New York, Teachers College Press.

FLEMING, K.G. (1976) 'The epistemological character of the relation between the concepts of teaching and learning', PhD Thesis, University of London.

FLEMING, K.G. (1980) 'Criteria of learning and teaching', *Journal of Philosophy of Education*, 14, 1.

FLEW, A. (1976) *Sociology, Equality and Education*, London, Macmillan.

GOODMAN, P. (1971) *Compulsory Miseducation*, Harmondsworth, Penguin.

GOW, K. (1980) *Yes Virginia, There is Right and Wrong*, Toronto, Wiley.

GRIBBLE, J. (1969) *Introduction to Philosophy of Education*, Boston, Allyn and Bacon.

HAMM, C.M. (1970) 'The logic of moral instruction', PhD Thesis. University of London.

HAMM, C.M. (1977) 'The content of moral education, or in defence of the "Bag of Virtues"' *The School Review*, February, pp. 218–28.

HAMM, C.M. (1986) 'Moral education and the distinction between social and personal morality' *Westminster Studies in Education*, 8, pp. 37–58.

HARE, W. (1979) *Open-Mindedness and Education*, Montreal, McGill-Queens University Press.

HARE, W. and PORTELLI, P. (Eds.) (1988) *Philosophy of Education: Introductory Readings*, Calgary, Detselig Enterprises Ltd.

HERSH, R., MILLER, J., and FIELDING, G. (1980) *Models of Moral Education*, New York, Longman.

HIRST, P.H. (1969) 'The logic of the curriculum' *Journal of Curriculum Studies*.

HIRST P.H. (1974) *Moral Education in a Secular Society*, London, University of London Press.

HIRST, P.H. (1974) *Knowledge and the Curriculum*, London, Routledge and Kegan Paul.

HIRST, P.H. and PETERS, R.S. (1970) *The Logic of Education*, London, Routledge and Kegan Paul.

HOLLINS, T.H.B. (1964) *Aims in Education*, Manchester, Manchester University Press.

HOOK, S. (1967) *Education for Modern Man*, New York, Alfred A. Knopf.

HUME, D. *Treatise on Human Nature* (any edition).

ILLICH, I. (1973) *Deschooling Society*, Harmondsworth, Penguin.

KANT, I. *Groundwork of the Metaphysics of Morals* (any edition).

KAZEPIDES, A.C. (1973) 'The grammar of indoctrination' *Philosophy of Education 1973: Proceedings of the Philosophy of Education Society*, University of Illinois.

KAZEPIDES, A.C. (1977) 'The logic of values clarification' *The Journal of Educational Thought*, 11, 2, pp. 99–111.

KAZEPIDES, A.C. (1978) 'On learning from the consequences of one's action', *Oxford Review of Education*, 4, 1, pp. 77–84.

KAZEPIDES, A.C. (1987) 'Indoctrination, doctrines, and the foundations of rationality', *Philosophy of Education: Proceeding of the Philosophy of Education Society*, University of Illinois.

KNELLER, G.F. (1964) *Introduction to Philosophy of Education*, New York, Wiley.

KOMISAR, B.P. and MACMILLAN, C.B.J. (Eds.) (1968) *Psychological Concepts in Education*, Chicago, Rand-McNally.

KOVESI, J. (1967) *Moral Notions*, London, Routledge and Kegan Paul.

LANGFORD, G. and O'CONNOR, D.J. (1973) *New Essays in the Philosophy of Education*, London, Routledge and Kegan Paul.

LLOYD, D.I. (Ed.) (1976) *Philosophy and the Teacher*, London, Routledge and Kegan Paul.

LORING, L.M. (1966) *Two Kinds of Value*, London, Routledge and Kegan Paul.

LUCAS, C.J. (Ed.) (1969) *What is Philosophy of Education?* London, Collier-Macmillan.

MACMILLAN, C.J.B. and NELSON, T.W. (Eds.) (1968) *Concepts of Teaching: Philosophical Essays*, Chicago, Rand McNally and Company.

MARTIN, J.R. (1970) *Explaining Understanding and Teaching*, New York, McGraw-Hill.

MCPECK, J. (1981) *Critical Thinking and Education*, Oxford, Martin Robertson.

MCPHAIL, P. (1982) *Social and Moral Education*, Oxford, Basil Blackwell.

MILNE, R.A. (1984) 'Moral development in early childhood', PhD Thesis, University of Melbourne.

MORGAN, J. (1985) 'Paul Hirst: Education as the development of rationality', MA Thesis, Simon Fraser University.

NEILL, A.S. (1968) *Summerhill*, Harmondsworth, Penguin.

O'CONNOR, D.J. (1975) *An Introduction to Philosophy of Education*, London, Routledge and Kegan Paul.

O'HEAR, A. (1981) *Education, Society and Human Nature*, London, Routledge and Kegan Paul.

OAKESHOTT, M. (1971) 'Education: The engagement and its frustration' *British Journal of Educational Studies*, V, 1, p. 46 ff.

OLSON, R.G. (1969) *Meaning and Argument: Elements of Logic*, New York, Harcourt Brace and World, Inc.

PASSMORE, J. (1980) *The Philosophy of Teaching*, Cambridge, Massachusetts, Harvard University Press.

PETERS, R.S. (1966) *Ethics and Education*, London, George Allen and Unwin.

PETERS, R.S. (Ed.) (1967) *The Concept of Education*, London, Routledge and Kegan Paul.

PETERS, R.S. (1973) *Authority, Responsibility and Education*, 3rd ed. London, Allen and Unwin.

PETERS, R.S. (Ed.) (1973) *The Philosophy of Education*, Oxford, University Press.

PETERS, R.S. (1974) *Psychology and Ethical Development*, London, George Allen and Unwin.

PHILLIPS, D.C. and SOLTIS, J.F. (1985) *Perspectives on Learning*, New York, Teachers College Press.

POSTMAN, N. and WEINGARTNER, C. (1971) *Teaching as a Subversive Activity*, Harmondsworth, Penguin.

PRING, R. (1976) *Knowledge and Schooling*, London, Open Books.

PRING, R. (1984) *Personal and Social Education in the Curriculum*, London, Hodder and Stoughton.

RATHS, L. *et al.* (1966) *Values and Teaching*, Columbus, Ohio, Charles E. Merrill.

REID, L.A. (1962) *Philosophy and Education*, London, Heineman.

RYLE, G. (1949) *The Concept of Mind*, New York, Barnes and Noble.

SCHEFFLER, I. (1960) *The Language of Education*, Springfield, Illinois, Charles C. Thomas.

SCHEFFLER, I (1965) *Conditions of Knowledge*, Glenview, Illinois, Scott, Foresman and Company.

SCHEFFLER, I. (Ed.) (1966) *Philosophy and Education: Modern Readings*, 2nd ed. Boston, Allyn and Bacon.

Bibliography

SCHEFFLER, I. (1973) *Reason and Teaching*, London, Routledge and Kegan Paul.

SCHEFFLER, I. (1987) *Of Human Potential: An Essay in Philosophy of Education*, London, Routledge and Kegan Paul.

SIEGEL, H. (1988) *Educating Reason*, New York, Routledge.

SIZER, N.F. and SIZER, J.R. (Eds.) (1970) *Moral Education: Five Lectures*, Cambridge, Harvard University Press.

SNOOK, I. (Ed.) (1972) *Concepts of Indoctrination*, London, Routledge and Kegan Paul.

SOLTIS, J. (1966) *Seeing, Knowing, and Believing*, London, George Allen and Unwin.

SOLTIS, J. (1985) *An Introduction to the Analysis of Educational Concepts*, 2nd ed. Reading, Massachusetts, Addison-Wesley Publishing Company.

STRIKE, K. and EGAN, K. (Eds.) (1978) *Ethics and Educational Policy*, London, Routledge and Kegan Paul.

STRIKE, K. and SOLTIS, J. (1985) *The Ethics of Teaching*, New York, Teachers College Press.

TAYLOR, D.M. (1970) *Explanation and Meaning*, Cambridge, University Press.

TAYLOR, W. (Ed.) (1984) *Metaphors of Education*, London, Heinemann.

TELFER, E. (1980) *Happiness*, London, Macmillan.

WALKER, D.F. and SOLTIS, J. (1986) *Curriculum and Aims*, New York, Teachers College Press.

WARNOCK, G.J. (1971) *The Object of Morality*, London, Methuen.

WARNOCK, M. (1977) *Schools of Thought*, London, Faber.

WATT, A.J. (1976) *Rational Moral Education*, Melbourne, University Press.

WHITE, J. (1973) *Towards a Compulsory Curriculum*, London, Routledge and Kegan Paul.

WHITE, J. (1982) *The Aims of Education Restated*, London, Routledge and Kegan Paul.

WHITE, P. (1983) *Beyond Domination: An Essary in the Political Philosophy of Education*, London, Routledge and Kegan Paul.

WILSON, J. (1970) *Moral Thinking*, London, Heineman.

WILSON, J. (1979) *Preface to the Philosophy of Education*, London, Routledge and Kegan Paul.

WILSON, J., WILLIAMS, N. and SUGARMAN, B. (1967) *Introduction to Moral Education*, Hammondsworth, Penguin.

WILSON, P.S. (1967) 'In defence of bingo', *British Journal of Educational Studies*, 15, February.

WRINGE, C. (1981) *Children's Rights*, London, Routledge and Kegan Paul.

YOUNG, M.F.D. (Ed.) (1971) *Knowledge and Control*, London, Collier-Macmillan.

Index

aims of education 44–5
  development of persons 45–50
  emphasis and imbalance 51
  moral *see* moral education
  school's role in society 53–7
  utility 52–3, 166–7
ambiguity 18, 19
art 73
assumptions 9–10
authority 77, 121–3
  student-teacher relationship
    personal relationships 124–6
    role relationship 123–4

belief 64–5
boredom
  justification of education 169–70
  unintended consequences of
    education 54
breadth of education 36–7

child-centered curricula 51, 76–8
  human nature considerations
    concept of 'human nature'
      83–4
    description of human nature
      84–6
    in education 86–8
  'needs' curriculum
    concept of 'need' 78–9
    motivation 81–2
    'needs' in educational
      curricula 79–80

    non-educational needs and the
      school 80–1
concepts and mental development
  46–7
conceptual analysis *see* meaning
conditioning 38, 39–40, 92
  distinguished from indoctrination
    100
consciousness 46–7
cultural renewal 24–6
  role of schools in society 55
  sociological definition of
    education 30
curriculum 59–60
  child-centered *see* child-centered
    curricula
  content 61–2
    principles for selection 88–9
  method 61
  nature of knowledge 62–4
    belief 64–5
    differentiation 67–73
    evidence 65–7
    truth 65
  objectives 62
  verifiable disciplines 46, 67–73

definitions 10–11
  programmatic 14–15
  reportive 13–14
  stipulative 12–13
deliberateness in education 33, 91,
  95
depth of education 37–8

descriptive definitions 13–14
deterrence 114–16
development of persons 45–50
discipline *see also* punishment
 definition 108–9
 forms 109–11

education
 aims *see* aims of education
 definition 29–30
  'general enlightenment' 31
  institutional 30–1
  R.S. Peters' analysis *see*
   Peters, R.S.
  sociological 30
 justification 163–5
  instrumental value 166–7
  intrinsic 169–73
  moral argument 165–6
  pleasure principle 167–8
 learning *see* learning
 moral *see* moral education
 physical 37, 55
 teaching *see* teaching
educational metaphors
 growth metaphor 20–4
 organic metaphor 24–6
educational theory 2–3
elitism 41–2
emotive language 18, 19
emphasis in education 51
empirical claims 8–9
empirical science 67, 68, 71
employability 54, 55, 166
encouragement 152–4
 reward 114
equality 41–2
errors of thought 8
essentialism 13
ethics 71 *see also* moral education
evidence 7–9, 65–7, 71
exemplification
 moral education 151–2
 student-teacher relationship 125
  discipline 110–111
experience 92

freedom 77
 definition 118–19

justification for infringement
 119–21

'general enlightenment' 31
 role of schools in society 55
growth metaphor 20–4

habit and moral training 146–8,
 153–4
'hidden curriculum' 54
Hirst, P. 46, 67–73
history 71, 85
human nature *see under* child-
 centered curricula

indoctrination 38, 39–40
 aims or intentions 101–2
 content 103–5
 method 100–1
 moral education 148
 results or manner 102–3
inequality 41–2, 56
initiation 33–4, 47
institutional definition of
 education 30–1
intellectualism 40–1, 72
intentionality in education 33,
 91, 95
 indoctrination 101–2

justification of education *see*
 under education

knowledge
 criterion for education 36–8,
  62–4
 belief 64–5
 evidence 65–7
 mastery 92–3
 truth 65
 forms of 46, 67–73
Kohlberg, L. 136–8, 149, 157

language
 ambiguity 18, 19
 emotive use 18, 19
 meaning *see* meaning
 metaphor 19–20
  growth metaphor 20–4

organic metaphor 24–6
vagueness 18
learning 91–3
  contingent connections with
    teaching 98–9
  logical connection with teaching
    and education 96–8
logical argument 8, 67, 71

mastery 92–3
mathematics 71, 73
meaning 5–7
  definitions 10–12
    programmatic 14–15
    reportive 13–14
    stipulative 12–13
mental development 45–50
metaphor 19–20
  growth metaphor 20–4
  organic metaphor 24–6
miseducation 99–100
  indoctrination *see*
    indoctrination
modelling
  moral education 151–2
  student-teacher relationship 125
    discipline 110–111
moral dilemmas 137, 148–51
moral education 128–9
  achievement of virtue 129, 136,
    146–7
  encouragement and reward
    114, 152–4
  enlightenment and instruction
    154–8
  exemplification 151–2 *see also*
    modelling
  habitual disposition and moral
    training 146–8
  Kohlberg's cognitive develop-
    mentalism 136–8, 149, 157
  moral dilemmas 137, 148–51
  paradoxical nature 158–9
  role of schools in society 55
  teaching specific moral content
    147–8
  theoretical bases
    basic values 142–3
    definition 138–142

rationality 143–5
values clarification 138
values education 129
motivation 81–2
  and discipline 110
music 73

naturalistic fallacy 23, 26, 86,
  113
necessary conditions 6–7
'needs' curriculum *see under*
  child-centered curricula
non-educational needs 80–1

organic metaphor 24–6

personal development 45–50
Peters, R.S.
  analysis of 'education' 32–4
    critical remarks 39–42
    elitism 41–2
    intellectualism 40–1
    knowledge criterion 36–8
    procedural criterion 38–9
    value (desirability) criterion
      34–5
philosophy
  definition 3–5
  evidence 7–9
  meaning *see* meaning
  of education 1–3
  presuppositions 9–10
physical education 37, 55, 165
potential 85–6
praise 152–3
predication 6
presuppositions 9–10
procedural criterion for education
  38–9
programmatic definitions 14–15
propositional knowledge 63–4
punishment *see also* discipline
  definition 111–13
  deterrence and prevention 114–16
  learning from consequences of
    actions 117–18
  moral education 152–4
  reform 116
  retribution 113–14

rationality 45–6, 49, 85, 170–3
  moral education 143–5
reform 116
relativity in ethics 138, 147–8
religion 72
reportive definitions 13–14
retribution 113–14
reward 114, 152–3

schools' role in society 53–7
science 67, 68, 71
socialization
  definition of education 30
  role of schools in society 53–7
stipulative definitions 12–13
student-teacher relationship
  personal relationships 124–6
  role relationship 123–4
subject-centered curriculum 59, 76
sufficient conditions 6–7

tabula rasa 46
teaching 93–4
  contingent connections with
    learning 98–9
  criteria 94–6

indoctrination *see*
  indoctrination
logical connection with learning
  96–8
miseducation 99–100
moral content 147–8
student-teacher relationship
  personal relationships 124–6
  role relationship 123–4
training 37
truth 65, 71

utilitarian aims of education
  52–3, 166–7

vagueness 18
value criterion for education 34–5,
  97
  aims of education *see* aims of
    education
  moral education *see* moral
    education
  the 'needs' curriculum 78, 81
verifiable educational disciplines
  46, 67–73
vocational training 165, 167 *see
  also* curriculum